LONDON

TOP SIGHTS · LOCAL EXPERIENCES

**DAMIAN HARPER, PETER DRAGICEVICH,
STEVE FALLON, EMILIE FILOU**

Contents

Plan Your Trip

London phone booth
PCRUCIATTI/SHUTTERSTOCK©

Explore London   41

Worth a Trip

Survival Guide   203

Special Features

Welcome to London

London has something for everyone, from art to grand museums, dazzling architecture, opulent royalty, striking diversity, glorious parks and irrepressible pizzazz. It's immersed in history, but London is also a tireless innovator of culture and creative talent. A cosmopolitan dynamism makes it quite possibly the world's most international city, yet one that remains somehow intrinsically British.

Regent's Park Open-air Theatre (p175)
VISITBRITAIN/SOHO NATHANIEL LEY IMAGES

Top Sights

British Museum

Britain's most visited attraction. **p88**

St Paul's Cathedral

Saintly symbol of London's resilience. **p108**

Tate Modern

A vigorous statement of modernity and architectural renewal. **p130**

Natural History Museum

Fascinating place of curatorial genius. **p152**

Tower of London

This imposing stone fortress is home to the Crown Jewels. **p112**

Westminster Abbey

Sacred place of coronation for England's sovereigns. **p44**

Houses of Parliament

There's no more iconic image of London than the Houses of Parliament and Big Ben. **p50**

National Gallery

One of the world's greatest art collections. **p66**

Victoria & Albert Museum

The world's largest decorative-arts collection. **p148**

Hampton Court Palace

The grandest Tudor palace in England. **p198**

LEFT © STONE/SHUTTERSTOCK © RIGHT: TOM GREEN/TOMGREENPHOTOS/500PX ©

LEFT: BENSON HE/SHUTTERSTOCK © RIGHT: PAJOR PAWEL/SHUTTERSTOCK ©

Buckingham Palace

The monarch's palatial London digs. **p48**

Royal Observatory & Greenwich Park

History, science and gorgeous views of London. **p192**

Eating

Once the butt of many a culinary joke, London has transformed itself over the last few decades and today is a global dining destination. World-famous chefs can be found at the helm of several top-tier restaurants, but it is the complete diversity on offer that is head-spinning: from Afghan to Zambian, London delivers an A to Z of world cuisine.

World Food

One of the joys of eating out in London is the sheer choice. For historical reasons Indian cuisine is widely available (curry has been labelled a national dish), but Asian cuisines in general are very popular. You'll find dozens of Chinese, Thai, Vietnamese Japanese and Korean restaurants, as well as elaborate fusion establishments blending flavours from different parts of Asia. Middle Eastern cuisine is also well covered. Continental Europe cuisines – French, Italian, Spanish, Greek, Scandinavian etc – are well represented, with many excellent modern European establishments. Restaurants serving ethnic cuisines tend to congregate where their home community is based.

British Food

Modern British food has become a cuisine in its own right, championing traditional (and sometimes underrated) ingredients such as root vegetables, smoked fish, shellfish, game, salt-marsh lamb, sausages, black pudding (a kind of sausage stuffed with oatmeal, spices and blood), offal, secondary cuts of meat and bone marrow.

Gastropubs

While not so long ago the pub was where you went for a drink, with maybe a packet of potato crisps to soak up the alcohol, the birth of the gastropub in the 1990s means that today just about every establishment serves full meals. The quality varies widely, from defrosted-on-the-premises to Michelin-star-worthy.

ROBIN STEWART/SHUTTERSTOCK ©

Best British

St John The restaurant that inspired the revival of British cuisine. (p121)

Dinner by Heston Blumenthal Winning celebration of British cuisine, with both traditional and modern accents. (p163)

Launceston Place Magnificent food, presentation and service. (p163)

Hook Camden Town What sort of British list would it be without fish and chips? (p176)

Best European

Padella Cheap and flavourful homemade pasta in Borough Market. (p139)

Club Gascon City restaurant showcasing the cuisine of France's southwest. (p121)

Tom's Kitchen Splendid service, seasonal European fare and a champion of sustainability. (p162)

Baltic Flavours from Eastern Europe on your plate, as well as in your glass. (p141)

Best Indian & Asian

Quilon London's most inventive Indian cuisine. (p60)

Gymkhana Splendid club-style Raj environment and top cuisine. (p60)

Hakkasan Hanway Place Superlative subterranean Cantonese den in the West End. (p100)

Miyama Gem of a Japanese restaurant with oodles of choice. (p120)

Kanada-Ya Join the queue for its superb *tonkotsu* ramen. (p76)

Top Tip

○ Many top-end restaurants offer set lunch menus that are great value.

○ The reliable internet booking service Open Table (www.opentable.co.uk) offers substantial discounts at selected restaurants.

London on a Plate
Pie & Mash

Mashed potato, creamy and smothered in sauce

Liquor, a parsley and vinegar sauce; if you don't like the sound of liquor, there is always gravy

The pie: minced beef for purists (variations allowed)

★ Top Spots for Pie & Mash

M Manze (www.manze.co.uk; 87 Tower Bridge Rd, SE1; mains from £2.95; ⏱11am-2pm Mon, 10.30am-2pm Tue-Thu, 10am-2.30pm Fri, to 2.45pm Sat; 🚇Borough)

Goddards at Greenwich (📞020-8305 9612; www.goddards atgreenwich.co.uk; 22 King William Walk, SE10; dishes £3.30-7.30; ⏱10am-7pm Sun-Thu, to 8pm Fri & Sat; 🚉DLR Cutty Sark)

F Cooke (📞020-7254 6548; 9 Broadway Market, E8; mains £2.70-4; ⏱10am-7pm Mon-Sat; 🚇London Fields)

Pie & Mash in London

From the middle of the 19th century until just after WWII, the staple lunch for many Londoners was a spiced-eel pie (eels were once plentiful in the Thames) served with mashed potatoes and liquor. The staple modern-day filling is minced beef (curried meat is also good). Pie-and-mash restaurants are rarely fancy, but they offer something of a time-travel culinary experience.

Meat pie with mushy peas.

Drinking & Nightlife

You need only glance at William Hogarth's Gin Lane prints from 1751 to realise that Londoners and alcohol have had more than a passing acquaintance. The metropolis offers a huge variety of venues to wet your whistle in – from cosy neighbourhood pubs to glitzy all-night clubs, and everything in between.

ALEX SEGRE/ALEXSEGRE/500PX ©

Pubs

At the heart of London social life, the pub (public house) is one of the capital's great social levellers. You can order almost anything you like, but beer is the staple. Some pubs specialise, offering drinks from local microbreweries, fruit beers, organic ciders and other rarer beverages. Others, especially gastropubs, proffer strong wine lists. Some pubs have delightful beer gardens – crucial in summer. Most pubs and bars open at 11am, closing at 11pm from Monday to Saturday and 10.30pm on Sunday. Some pubs stay open longer, often until midnight, sometimes 1am or 2am.

Bars & Clubs

Bars are generally open later than pubs but close earlier than clubs. They may have DJs and a small dance floor, door charges after 11pm, more modern decor and fancier (and pricier) drinks, including cocktails, than pubs. If you're up for clubbing, London is an embarrassment of riches: choose between legendary establishments such as Fabric or smaller clubs with up-and-coming DJs. Dress to impress (no jeans or trainers) in posh clubs in areas such as Kensington. Further east, it's laid back and edgy. Cocktail bars are undergoing a renaissance, so you'll find lots of upmarket options serving increasingly interesting concoctions.

Best Pubs

Edinboro Castle Cultured Primrose Hill boozer with a beer garden. (p177)

Lock Tavern Top Camden pub with a roof terrace and live music. (p178)

PYMCA/UIG/AGE FOTOSTOCK ©

Ye Olde Mitre Cosy, historic pub with a great beer selection and no music – how civilised. (p123)

Windsor Castle High up on the brow of Kensington's Campden Hill Rd, with a fabulous beer garden. (p164)

Best Historic Pubs

George Inn History, age-old charm and National Trust designation. (p142)

Jerusalem Tavern An 18th-century ale-aficionado's bolthole. (p124)

Lamb & Flag Atmospheric and creaky old-timer from days of yore, near the Strand. (p80)

Best Bars

American Bar Dapper art-deco stunner at the Beaumont Hotel in the West End. (p79)

Sky Pod Drinks always taste better with views. (p123)

Dukes London Classic bar at the heart of London with the best Martinis in town. (p61)

Oblix Stellar views of London across the river from the 32nd floor of the Shard. (p142)

Best Clubs

Fabric London's most famous superclub. (pictured above; p124)

Heaven *The* gay club in London. (p81)

Online Listings

Check the listings in *Time Out* (www.time out.com/london) or the *Evening Standard*. Part of the charm of London's nightlife is that it's always changing, so keep your eyes peeled.

London in a Glass
Pimm's & Lemonade

Sunshine, shades and good company to serve

One part Pimm's, three parts lemonade

Highball glass (not a pint, this is a classy drink) and ice

For additional flourish, lemon, lime and cucumber slices

Strawberries, orange and fresh mint – the bare minimum

ERAINBOW/SHUTTERSTOCK ©

★ Top Three Places for Pimm's

Edinboro Castle (www.edinboro castlepub.co.uk; 57 Mornington Tce, NW1; ◷noon-11pm Mon-Sat, noon-10.30pm Sun; 🛜; ⊖Camden Town)

Spaniards Inn (www.thespaniards innhampstead.co.uk; Spaniards Rd, NW3; ◷noon-11pm; 🛜 👪; 🚌 210)

Windsor Castle (www.thewindsor castlekensington.co.uk; 114 Camp-den Hill Rd, W11; ◷noon-11pm Mon-Sat, to 10.30pm Sun; 🛜; ⊖Notting Hill Gate)

Pimm's & Lemonade in London

Pimm's, a gin-based fruity spirit, is the quintessential British summer drink: no sunny afternoon in a beer garden would be complete without a glass (or a jug) of it. It is served with lemonade, mint and fresh fruit. Most pubs and bars serve it, although they may only have all the trimmings in summer.

Traditional Pimm's

BBA PHOTOGRAPHY/SHUTTERSTOCK ©

Shopping

From charity-shop finds to designer bags, there are thousands of ways to spend your hard-earned cash in London. Many of the big-name shopping attractions, such as Harrods, Hamleys and Camden Market, have become must-sees in their own right. Chances are that with so many temptations, you'll give your wallet a full workout.

EDMUND SUMNER-VIEW/ALAMY STOCK PHOTO ©

Chain Stores

Many bemoan the fact that chains have taken over the main shopping centres, leaving independent shops struggling to balance the books. But since they're cheap, fashionable and always conveniently located, Londoners (and others) keep going back for more. As well as familiar overseas retailers, such as Gap, H&M, Urban Outfitters and Zara, you'll find plenty of home-grown chains, including luxury womenswear brand Karen Millen (www.karenmillen.com) and global giant Topshop (www.topshop.co.uk).

Opening Hours

London shops generally open from 9am or 10am to 6pm or 7pm, Monday to Saturday. The majority of West End (Oxford St, Soho and Covent Garden), Chelsea, Knightsbridge, Kensington, Greenwich and Hampstead shops also open on Sunday, typically from noon to 6pm, but sometimes 10am to 4pm. Shops in the West End open late (to 9pm) on Thursday; those in Chelsea, Knightsbridge and Kensington open late on Wednesday. If a major market is in swing on a certain day, neighbouring shops will probably also fling open their doors.

Best Shopping Areas

West End Grand confluence of big names for the well heeled and well dressed.

Knightsbridge Harrods and other top names servicing London's wealthiest residents.

NATALYA OKOROKOVA ©

Best Department Stores

Harrods Garish, stylish and just this side of kitsch, yet perennially popular. (pictured above; p165)

Liberty An irresistible blend of contemporary styles in an old-fashioned mock-Tudor atmosphere. (p84)

Fortnum & Mason London's oldest grocery store with staff still dressed in old-fashioned attire (p83)

Best Bookshops

John Sandoe Books Fine, knowledgeable customer service and terrific stock in one of London's most charming shops. (p165)

Hatchards London's oldest bookshop (1797), with fantastic stock and plenty of events. (p83)

Waterstones Piccadilly Europe's largest bookshop, with well-read staff and regular author readings and signings. (p84)

London Review Bookshop Strong and choice literary selection. (p105)

Best for Gifts

Penhaligon's Beautiful range of perfumes and home fragrances, overseen by very helpful staff. (pictured above left; p84)

London Silver Vaults Beautifully crafted silver artefacts, from tableware to jewellery. (p125)

Lovely & British Bermondsey boutique with British-designed prints, jewellery and ceramics. (p145)

Tax-Exempt Purchases

In stores displaying a 'tax free' sign, visitors from non-EU countries are entitled to claim back the 20% VAT on purchases. See www.gov.uk/tax-on-shopping/taxfree-shopping.

Top London Souvenirs

WENN LTD/ALAMY STOCK PHOTO ©

Music

London is brilliant for buying records. Try Rough Trade East (p191) in Spitalfields.

London Toys

Double-decker buses, Paddington bears, guards in bearskin hats, London's icons make for great souvenirs. Hamleys (p85) is the place to go.

TIWAKORN DHUPAGUPTA/SHUTTERSTOCK ©

EURASIA PRESS/GETTY IMAGES ©

Tea

The British drink par excellence, with plenty of iconic names to choose from. For lovely packaging too, try Fortnum & Mason (pictured; p83) or Harrods (p165).

PAOLO PARADISO/SHUTTERSTOCK ©

Vintage Clothes & Shoes

Your London vintage fashion finds will forever be associated with your trip to the city. Start your search at Old Spitalfields Market (pictured; p191) or the Sunday UpMarket (p185) in the East End.

MATTHEW TAYLOR/ALAMY STOCK PHOTO ©

Collectable Books

London is heaven for bibliophiles, with numerous history-filled bookshops, brimming with covet-table first editions and hard-to-find signed tomes. Try Hatchards (pictured; p83) or John Sandoe Books (p165).

Entertainment

Whatever it is that sets your spirits soaring or your booty shaking, you'll find it in London. The city's been a world leader in theatre ever since a young man from Stratford-upon-Avon set up shop here in the 16th century. And if London started swinging in the 1960s, its live rock and pop scene has barely let up since.

Theatre

A night out at the theatre is as much a must-do London experience as a trip on the top deck of a double-decker bus. London's Theatreland in the dazzling West End – from Aldwych in the east, past Shaftesbury Ave to Regent St in the west – has a concentration of theatres only rivalled by New York's Broadway.

Classical Music

With multiple world-class orchestras and ensembles, quality venues, reasonable ticket prices and performances covering the whole musical gamut from traditional crowd-pleasers to innovative compositions, London will satisfy even the fussiest classical music buff.

London Sounds

London has long generated edgy and creative sounds. There's live music – rock, blues, jazz, folk, whatever – going on every night of the week in steaming clubs, crowded pubs or ear-splitting concert arenas.

Best Theatre

Shakespeare's Globe For the authentic open air Elizabethan effect. (p143)

National Theatre Cutting-edge productions in a choice of three theatres. (pictured; p144)

Best for Classical Music & Opera

Royal Albert Hall Splendid red-brick Victorian concert hall south of Kensington Gardens. (p164)

Royal Opera House The venue of choice for classical ballet and opera buffs. (p82)

MILAN GONDA/SHUTTERSTOCK ©

Best Live Jazz

Ronnie Scott's Legendary Frith St jazz club in the heart of the West End. (p82)

Pizza Express Jazz Club Top-class jazz in the basement of a chain restaurant. (p81)

Jazz Cafe Much more than just jazz these days, but still staging some of London's best jams. (p178)

Best Live Rock & Pop

KOKO Fabulously glitzy venue, showcasing original indie rock. (p178)

Royal Albert Hall Gorgeous, grand and spacious, yet strangely intimate. (p164)

Best Music in Churches

Westminster Abbey Evensong and the city's finest organ concerts. (p53)

St Paul's Cathedral Evensong at its most evocative. (p108)

St Martin-in-the-Fields Excellent classical music concerts, many by candlelight. (p74)

Best Dance

Southbank Centre From Bollywood to break-dancing, and all things in between. (p138)

The Place The very birthplace of modern English dance. (p104)

Standby Tickets

Cut-price standby tickets are generally available at the National Theatre, the Barbican, the Southbank Centre and the Royal Opera House. Pick up in person on the day. Cheap £5 standing tickets are available daily at Shakespeare's Globe.

Museums & Galleries

London's museums and galleries top the list of the city's top attractions and not just for the rainy days that frequently send locals scurrying for cover. Some of London's museums and galleries display incomparable collections that make them acknowledged leaders in their field.

Admission & Access

National museum collections (eg British Museum, National Gallery, Victoria & Albert Museum) are free, except for temporary exhibitions. Private galleries are usually free (or have a small admission fee), while smaller museums will charge an entrance fee, typically around £5 (book online for discounted tickets at some museums). National collections are generally open 10am to around 6pm, with one late night a week.

Museums at Night

Evenings are an excellent time to visit museums, as there are far fewer visitors. Many museums open late once a week, and several organise special nocturnal events to extend their range of activities and present the collection in a different mood. Hop onto museum websites to see what's in store. (Some only arrange night events once a year, in May).

Specialist Museums

Whether you've a penchant for fans, London transport or ancient surgical techniques, you'll discover museums throughout the city with their own niche collections. Even for non-specialists, these museums can be fascinating to browse and to share in the enthusiasm that's instilled in the collections by their curators.

Best Collections (All Free)

British Museum Supreme collection of rare artefacts. (pictured; p88)

KIEV.VICTOR/SHUTTERSTOCK ©

Victoria & Albert Museum
Unique array of decorative arts and design in an awe-inspiring setting. (p148)

National Gallery Tremendous gathering of largely pre-modern masters. (p66)

Tate Modern A feast of modern and contemporary art, wonderfully housed. (p130)

Natural History Museum Major hit with kids and adults alike. (p152)

Best House Museums

Sir John Soane's Museum Bewitching museum brimming with 18th-century curiosities. (p72)

Dennis Severs' House Home of a Huguenot silk weaver's family, preserved as if still inhabited. (p187)

Best Museum Architecture

Victoria & Albert Museum A building as beautiful as its diverse collection. (p148)

Natural History Museum Architectural lines straight from a Gothic fairy tale. (p152)

Best Small Museums

Old Operating Theatre Museum & Herb Garret Unique, eye-opening foray into old-fashioned surgery techniques. (p138)

Museum of Brands, Packaging & Advertising Riveting collection of brand names through the ages, in Notting Hill. (p167)

Museum Bites 🍽️

Many of the top museums also have fantastic restaurants, worthy of a visit in their own right.

Architecture

London is dotted with architectural gems from every period of its long history. This is a city for explorers: keep your eyes peeled and you'll spot part of a Roman wall enclosed in the lobby of a postmodern building near St Paul's, or a galleried coaching inn dating from the Restoration tucked away in a courtyard off a high street in Borough.

London Style

Unlike certain other cities, London has never been methodically planned. Instead, it has developed in an almost haphazard fashion. As a result, London retains architectural reminders from every period of its long history, but they are often hidden: part of a Roman wall enclosed in the lobby of a modern building near St Paul's Cathedral, say, or a galleried coaching inn from the Restoration in a courtyard off Borough High St.

Best Modern Icons

Cheese Grater Opened in mid-2014, the 225m-tall Leadenhall Building in the form of a stepped wedge faces architect Richard Rogers' other icon, the Lloyd's of London building.

The Gherkin The 180m-tall bullet-shaped tower that seems to pop up at every turn; aka 30 St Mary Axe.

The Shard Needle-like 87-storey tower by Italian architect Renzo Piano, with awesome views from its top floors. (p139)

Walkie Talkie This 37-storey, 160m-tall tower bulges in and bulges out. Visit the Sky Garden to experience the City's sixth-tallest building. (p118)

Trellis (1 Undershaft, Bishopsgate) Reaching completion at press time, the 305m-tall 1 Undershaft will be the City of London's tallest building.

Best Early Architecture

Westminster Abbey Titanic milestone in London's ecclesiastical architectural history. (p53)

Houses of Parliament Westminster Hall has one of the finest hammerbeam roofs in the world. (p53)

Tower of London Legend, myth and bloodstained history converge in London's supreme bastion. (p112)

All Hallows by the Tower Fragments from Roman times in one of London's oldest churches. (p119)

MICHELE PRISCO/MICHELEPRISCO/500PX ©

Best Stately Architecture

Buckingham Palace
The Queen's pied-à-terre.
(p53)

Houses of Parliament
Extraordinary Victorian
monument and seat of British parliamentary democ-
racy. (p53)

Queen's House Beautiful
Inigo Jones Palladian creation in charming Greenwich.
(p195)

Hampton Court Palace
Get lost in the famous maze
or ghost hunt along Tudor
hallways. (p198)

Old Royal Naval College
Admire the stunning Painted
Hall and breathtaking
chapel. (p197)

Best Monuments

Monument Spiral your way
to the top for panoramic
views. (p118)

Albert Memorial Convoluted
and admirably excessive
chunk of Victoriana. (p158)

Marble Arch Huge white
arch designed by John Nash.
(p160)

Open House Architectural Tours

For one weekend at the end of September, hundreds of buildings
normally closed to the public throw open their doors for **Open
House London** (☎020-7383 2131; www.openhouselondon.org.uk). Public
buildings aren't forgotten either, with plenty of talks and tours. This
architectural charity also sponsors talks with architectural tours
to various areas of London held by sister organisation **Open City**
(☎020-3006 7008; www.open-city.org.uk; tours £24.50-35.50).

For Kids

London is a fantastic place for children. The city's museums will fascinate all ages, and you'll find theatre, dance and music performances ideal for older kids. Playgrounds and parks, city farms and nature reserves are perfect for either toddler energy-busting or relaxation.

Museum Activities

London's museums are very child friendly, with dedicated children or family trails in virtually every one. Additionally, you'll find plenty of activities such as storytelling at the National Gallery, thematic backpacks to explore the British Museum, pop-up performances at the Victoria & Albert Museum, family audio guides at the Tate Modern, and art and crafts workshops at Somerset House, where kids can dance through the fountains in the courtyard in summer. The Science Museum has a marvellous interactive area downstairs called the Garden, where tots can splash around with water.

Eating with Kids

Many London restaurants and cafes are child-friendly and offer baby-changing facilities and high chairs. Pick your places with some awareness – avoid high-end and quieter restaurants if you have toddlers or babies. Note that gastropubs tend to be very family-friendly, but that drinking-only pubs may not allow children under the age of 16. If a children's menu isn't available, just ask for a smaller portion, which most restaurants will be happy to provide.

Best Sights for Kids

ZSL London Zoo Close to 750 species of animals and an excellent Penguin Beach. (p174)

London Eye Survey London from altitude and tick off the big sights. (p136)

London Dungeon Squeam-ish fun, London's famous

PPTARA/SHUTTERSTOCK ©

villains and chilling thrills. (p137)

Madame Tussauds Selfie heaven, be it with One Direction or Darth Vader. (p174)

Changing of the Guard Soldiers in bearskin hats, red uniforms and military orders: kids will gape. (p56)

Cutty Sark Explore a real ship and learn about its history sailing the high seas. (p197)

Best Museums for Kids

Science Museum Bursting with imaginative distractions for technical tykes, plus a fun-filled basement for little ones. (p158)

Imperial War Museum Packed with exciting displays, warplanes and military whatnot. (p137)

British Museum Meet the mummies at London's best museum. (p88)

Natural History Museum Gawp at the overhanging Blue Whale skeleton and animatronic T rex. (p152)

Best for Babies & Toddlers

Kensington Gardens Fantastic playground, a fountain to splash about in, and hectares of greenery to explore. (p160)

St James's Park Ducks, squirrels and pelicans in the shadow of Buckingham Palace. (p57)

Top Tips for Families

○ Under-11s travel free on all public transport, except National Rail services.

○ In winter months (November to January), ice rinks appear at the Natural History Museum, Somerset House and Hampton Court.

Tours

JEFF WHYTE/SHUTTERSTOCK ©

Best Boat Tours

Thames River Services
(📞020-7930 4097; www.
thamesriverservices.
co.uk; adult/child one-
way £12.50/6.25, return
£16.50/8.25) Cruise boats
leave Westminster Pier for
Greenwich, stopping at the
Tower of London.

Thames Rockets (📞020-
7928 8933; www.thames-
rockets.com; Boarding Gate
1, London Eye, Waterloo
Millennium Pier, Westmin-
ster Bridge Rd, SE1; adult/
child from £43.50/29.50;
⏰10am 6pm; 👶) Tear
through London on a high-
speed inflatable boat in true
James Bond fashion.

Thames River Boats
(📞020-7930 2062; www.
wpsa.co.uk; Westminster Pier,
Victoria Embankment, SW1;
Kew adult/child one-way
£13/6.50, return £20/10,
Hampton Court one-way
£17/8.50, return £25/12.50;
⏰10am-4pm Apr-Oct;
🚇Westminster) Cruise from

Westminster Pier to the Royal
Botanic Gardens at Kew
(1½ hours) and/or Hampton
Court Palace (another 1½
hours), with a chance to
disembark at Richmond, if
the tide's right.

Best Walking Tours

Guide London (Association of Professional Tourist
Guides; 📞020-7611 2545;
www.guidelondon.org.uk;
half-/full day £165/270)
Prestigious and super-
knowledgeable Blue Badge
Tourist Guides who really
know their stuff.

London Walks (📞020-
7624 3978; www.walks.com;
adult/child £10/free) Large
choice of themed walks to
cover just about any procliv-
ity, from ghost tours, to
Beatles tours, Harry Potter
and Sherlock Holmes.

Unseen Tours (📞07514
266774; www.sockmob
events.org.uk; tours £12)
London from a different

perspective, led by homeless
people, covering Camden
Town, Brick Lane, Shoreditch
and London Bridge.

Strawberry Tours (📞020-
7859 4996; www.straw-
berrytours.com/london)
Operates on a 'pay what you
feel' basis, on a variety of
themes.

Best Bus Tours

Big Bus Tours (📞020-
7808 6753; www.bigbus-
tours.com; adult/child
£35/18; ⏰every 20min
8.30am-6pm Apr-Sep, to
5pm Oct & Mar, to 4.30pm
Nov-Feb) Informative com-
mentaries in 12 languages.
Ticket includes a free river
cruise and three thematic
walking tours.

Original Tour (www.the
originaltour.com; adult/child
£32/15; ⏰8.30am-8.30pm)
Open-top hop-on, hop-off 24-
hour bus tour, complete with
river cruise and thematic
walking tours. Buses run
every five to 20 minutes.

Festivals & Events

London is a vibrant city year-round, celebrating both traditional and modern festivals and events with energy and gusto. From Europe's largest outdoor carnival to the blooms of the Chelsea Flower Show and the pomp and ceremony of Trooping the Colour, London has entertaining occasions for all tastes.

BEN GINGELL/SHUTTERSTOCK ©

Best Free Festivals

Notting Hill Carnival (www. thelondonnottinghillcarnival.com) London's most vibrant outdoor carnival is a celebration of Caribbean London; in August.

Chinese New Year Chinatown fizzes in this colourful street festival in late January or February.

Trooping the Colour The Queen's official birthday in June sees parades and pageantry at Horse Guards Parade.

Guy Fawkes' Night (Bonfire Night) Commemorates Guy Fawkes' attempt to blow up parliament in 1605, with bonfires and fireworks across London on 5 November.

Lord Mayor's Show (www. lordmayorsshow.org) Floats, bands and fireworks to celebrate the Lord Mayor in November.

London Marathon Around 40,000 runners pound through London in April in one of the world's biggest road races.

Best Ticketed Events

Tennis Championships (www.wimbledon.com) Centre of the tennis universe for two weeks in June/July.

The Proms (www.bbc.co.uk/ proms) Classical concerts around the Royal Albert Hall from July to September.

London Film Festival (www. bfi.org.uk/lff) Premier film event held at the BFI Southbank and other venues in October.

Chelsea Flower Show (www.rhs.org.uk/chelsea) Renowned horticultural show, attracting the cream of West London society in May.

Events Listings Online

For a list of events in and around London, check www.visitlondon.com or www.timeout.com/london.

LGBTIQ+ London

The city of Oscar Wilde, Quentin Crisp and Elton John does not disappoint its LGBTIQ+ visitors, proffering a fab mix of brash, camp, loud and edgy parties, bars, clubs and events year-round. It's a world capital of gaydom, on par with New York and San Francisco – London's LGBTIQ+ communities have turned good times into an art form.

KATIE STEVENS PHOTOGRAPHY/SHUTTERSTOCK ©

LGBTIQ+ London by Neighbourhood

Cool Shoreditch is home to London's more alternative LGBTIQ+ scene. The long-established gay village of Soho has lost some ground to the edgy East End. Vauxhall in South London is where to go for the biggest club nights.

Bars & Clubs

That said, London still has a widely varied bar scene with venues spread across the city, not just in the traditional Soho heartland.

Best Events

BFI Flare (www.bfi.org.uk/llgff) Hosted by the BFI in early April, with premieres, screenings and talks.

Pride in London (http://prideinlondon.org) In late June/early July; one of the world's largest gay pride events.

Best Clubs & Shops

Heaven Long-standing club and still a Saturday night magnet on the gay scene. (p81)

Gay's the Word Excellent range of LGBT-interest books and magazines. (p105)

LGBTIQ+ Event Listings

Check out www.gingerbeer.co.uk for the full low-down on lesbian events, club nights and bars. Also click on 60by80 (www.60by80.com/london) for gay travel information and Time Out London LGBT (www.timeout.com/london/lgbt) for bar, club and events listings.

Markets

ANNA LEVAN/SHUTTERSTOCK ©

London Life

Shopping at London's markets isn't just about picking up bargains and rummaging through mounds of knick-knacks – although they give you plenty of opportunity to do that. It's also about taking in the character of this vibrant city: Londoners love to trawl through markets – browsing, chatting and socialising.

Lunch on the Side

Food stalls and/or food trucks are a feature of London markets, whether or not the markets specialise in food. They generally do a roaring trade, thanks to hungry shoppers keen to sit and take in the buzz. The quality varies, but is generally good, and the prices are reasonable (£4 to £8).

Best Markets

Borough Market Bustling cornucopia of gastronomic delights, south of the river. (pictured above; p136)

Old Spitalfields Market Huge, sprawling market on the border of the City and the East End, excellent for vintage and fashion. (p191)

Camden Market North London's must-see market, with everything from authentic antiques to tourist tat. (p174)

Portobello Market London's best-known market, in ever-hip Notting Hill. perfect for vintage everything. (p167)

Brick Lane Market Sunday confluence of bric-a-brac, cheap clothes and street eats. (p185)

Sunday UpMarket Load up on delicious food before tackling the designer stalls. (p185)

Borough Market Top Tip

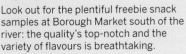

Look out for the plentiful freebie snack samples at Borough Market south of the river: the quality's top-notch and the variety of flavours is breathtaking.

Four Perfect Days

Day 1

LUKASZ PAJOR/SHUTTERSTOCK ©

First stop, **Trafalgar Sq** (p72) for its architectural grandeur and photo-op views of **Big Ben** (p51). Then head indoors to the **National Gallery** (p66) to admire Van Gogh's *Sunflowers*. Press on to **Westminster Abbey** (p53) to immerse yourself in its ecclesiastical and royal history.

For gourmet cuisine at budget prices, stop by the **Vincent Rooms** (p59) for lunch. Cross the river on Westminster Bridge to the **London Eye** (p136). Continue along the South Bank to the **Tate Modern** (p130) for some A-grade modern art.

Wind down with a drink in the historic **George Inn** (p142) and enjoy dinner at **Arabica Bar & Kitchen** (p142) at the heart of the historic **Borough Market** (p136).

Day 2

JOHN CROUX/SHUTTERSTOCK ©

Get to the **Tower of London** (p112) early (8.50am) to witness the **Unlocking of the Tower** and spend the morning marvelling at the **Crown Jewels**. Then take some time to admire the iconic **Tower Bridge** (p63) on the Thames.

Make your way to **St Paul's Cathedral** (p108) to explore the exquisite architecture and dome. Hop on a bus to **Covent Garden** and take in the buzz. Continue to **Leicester Sq** (p81) with its cinemas and film premieres and **Piccadilly Circus** (p73) and its famous statue.

After all this traipsing, stop by **Dukes London** (p61) for a relaxing Martini, followed by delectable Jerusalem cuisine at **Palomar** (p76). Stay in Piccadilly and Soho for a nightcap pint at the **Lamb & Flag** (p80).

Day 3

MIBIG2/SHUTTERSTOCK ©

Devote a couple of hours to the **British Museum** (p88). Round out the morning with a stroll around **Bloomsbury**, once the undisputed centre of the literary world.

Enjoy a tasty sandwich or afternoon tea at **Tea & Tattle** (p89), before heading to the upmarket borough of Chelsea and Kensington for (window) shopping. **Harrods** (p165) is a must for gourmet souvenirs. Round off the day with a stroll around **Hyde Park** (p158).

Come night, the buzzing nightlife of **Camden** awaits you. Enjoy marvellous sustainable fish and chips at **Hook Camden Town** (p176) before letting the live music kick in: for indie rock, **KOKO** (p178); for jazz, wend your way to **Jazz Cafe** (p178).

Day 4

STOYANH/SHUTTERSTOCK ©

Hop on a boat in central London and float down the Thames to Greenwich, and take our **Greenwich walk** (p196). Explore the **National Maritime Museum** (p197), **Queen's House** (p195) and the **Cutty Sark** (p197). **Greenwich Market** (p197) can sort lunch.

Stroll through **Greenwich Park** (p195) all the way up to the **Royal Observatory** (p192). The views unfolding below you to **Canary Wharf** are magnificent. Inside the observatory, straddle the **Greenwich Meridian** and learn about the incredible quest to solve the longitude problem.

Have a pint and a British dinner at the picture-postcard **Trafalgar Tavern** (p197) before heading to the City for a panoramic drink at **Sky Pod** (p123).

Need to Know

For detailed information, see Survival Guide (p203)

Language
English (and more than 300 others)

Currency
Pound sterling (£)

Visas
Not required for Australian, Canadian, New Zealand and US visitors, for stays of up to six months.

Money
ATMs are widespread. Major credit cards are accepted everywhere.

Mobile Phones
Buy local SIM cards for European and Australian phones, or a pay-as-you-go phone.

Time
London is on GMT/UTC.

Tipping
Hotels: £1 per bag.
Restaurants: 15% for exceptional service.
Pubs: not expected unless table service is provided; no need to tip at the bar.
Taxis: round the fare up to the nearest pound.

Daily Budget

Budget: Less than £85
Dorm bed: £12–30
Market-stall lunch or supermarket sandwich: £3.50–5
Many museums: free
Standby theatre tickets: £5–25
Santander Cycles daily rental fee: £2

Midrange: £85–200
Double room: £100–200
Two-course dinner with glass of wine: £35
Temporary exhibitions: £12–18
Theatre tickets: £15–60

Top end: More than £200
Four-star or boutique hotel room: more than £200
Three-course dinner in top restaurant with wine: £60–90
Black cab trip: £30
Top theatre tickets: £65

Advance Planning

Three months before Book weekend performances for top shows; make dinner reservations at renowned restaurants; snap up tickets for must-see temporary exhibitions; book accommodation.

One month before Check listings on entertainment sites such as *Time Out* (www.timeout.com/london) for fringe theatre, live music and festivals, and book tickets.

A few days before Check the weather online through the Met Office (www.metoffice.gov.uk).

Arriving in London

Most people arrive in London by air, but an increasing number of visitors coming from Europe take the train.

✈ From Heathrow Airport

Trains, the tube and buses to London from just after 5am to before midnight and cost £5.70 to £21.50; taxi £46 to £87.

✈ From Gatwick Airport

Trains to London from 4.30am to 1.35am cost £10 to £20; hourly buses to London 24/7, from £5; taxi £100.

✈ From Stansted Airport

Trains to London from 5.30am to 1.30am cost £23.40; 24/7 buses to London from £12; taxi from £130.

✈ From Luton Airport

Trains to London from 7am to 10pm from £14; buses 24/7 to London, £10; taxi £110.

🚉 St Pancras International Train Station

In Central London (for Eurostar train arrivals from Europe) and connected by many underground lines to other parts of the city.

Getting Around

The cheapest way to get around London is with an Oyster Card (see p208) or a UK contactless card.

⊖ Tube, Overground & DLR

The London Underground ('the tube'), Overground and DLR are, overall, the quickest and easiest ways to get about the city, if not the cheapest.

🚌 Bus

The bus network is extensive but slow-going except for short hops. Fares are good value if used with an Oyster card and there are plentiful night buses and 24-hour routes.

🚖 Taxi

Black-cab drivers always know where they are going, but fares are steep unless you're in a group. Minicabs are cheaper, but must be booked in advance.

🚲 Bicycle

Santander Cycles (p209) are ideal for shorter journeys around central London.

🚗 Car & Motorcycle

As a visitor, it's unlikely you'll need to drive in London. Disincentives include extortionate parking charges, congestion charges, traffic jams, the high price of petrol, efficient traffic wardens and wheel clamps.

Useful Websites

Lonely Planet (www.lonelyplanet.com/england/london) Destination information, hotelbookings, traveller forum and more.
Time Out London (www.timeout.com/london) Up-to-date and comprehensive entertainment listings distributed for free every Tuesday.
Londonist (www.londonist.com) A website about London and everything that happens in it.

London Neighbourhoods

Regent's Park & Camden (p169)
North London has a strong accent on nightlife, parkland and heaths, canal-side charm, markets and international menus.

National Gallery & Covent Garden (p65)
Bright lights, big city: West End theatres, big-ticket museums, fantastic restaurants, shopping galore and boho nightlife.

Buckingham Palace

Natural History Museum

Victoria & Albert Museum

Kensington Museums (p147)
One of London's classiest neighbourhoods with fine museums, hectares of parkland and top-grade shopping and dining.

Westminster Abbey & Westminster (p43)
The royal and political heart of London: pomp, pageantry and history in spades, and home to a number of London's biggest attractions.

British Museum & Bloomsbury (p87)
London's most famous museum, elegant squares, eclectic dining and literary pubs.

Shoreditch & the East End (p183)
London's creative and clubbing energy fills Shoreditch with history, museums, ace eats and markets aplenty in the East End.

British Museum

National Gallery

St Paul's Cathedral

Tate Modern

Tower of London

Houses of Parliament

Westminster Abbey

St Paul's & the City (p107)
London's iconic church and tower are here, alongside ancient remains, historic churches, architectural gems and hearty pubs.

Tate Modern & South Bank (p129)
Modern art, innovative theatre, Elizabethan drama, superb dining, modern architecture and traditional pubs.

Royal Observatory & Greenwich Park

Explore
London

Worth a Trip 👀

London's Walking Tours 🚶

Poppie's (p188) DOSFOTOS DOSFOTOS/GETTY IMAGES ©

Explore ◉
Westminster Abbey & Westminster

Westminster is the political heart of London, and the level of pomp and circumstance here is astounding – state occasions are marked by convoys of gilded carriages, elaborate parades and, in the case of the opening of parliament, by a man in a black coat banging on the front door with a jewelled sceptre. Tourists flock here to marvel at Buckingham Palace and the neo-Gothic Houses of Parliament.

Get queuing at Westminster Abbey (p44) early in the day to thwart the crowds. You'll want to spend most of the morning here admiring its mighty stonework, exploring the cloisters and the abbey's historic grandeur. Head to St James's Park (p53) for some greenery at lunchtime and choose between a picnic on the grass or a meal at Vincent Rooms (p59). After lunch, walk to grand Buckingham Palace (p48) in summer or the Houses of Parliament (p50) during the rest of the year (when parliament is sitting). Dine at Gymkhana (p60) for superb Indian fare before rounding off the evening with a delightful cocktail at classic Dukes London (p61) or the opulent Rivoli Bar (p61) at the Ritz.

Getting There & Around

◉ Westminster and St James's Park are both on the Circle and District Lines. The Jubilee Line runs through Westminster and Green Park; the latter station is also a stop on the Piccadilly and Victoria Lines.

Westminster Map on p54

Big Ben clock tower ALEXEY FEDORENKO/SHUTTERSTOCK ©

Top Sight 📷
Westminster Abbey

Westminster Abbey is such an important com- memoration site that it's hard to overstress its symbolic value or imagine its equivalent anywhere else in the world. Except for Edward V (murdered) and Edward VIII (abdicated), every English sovereign has been crowned here since William the Conqueror in 1066, many were mar- ried here and a total of 17 are buried here.

◎ **MAP P54, E5**

www.westminster-abbey.org

20 Dean's Yard, SW1

adult/child £22/9, cloister & gardens free

🕙 9.30am-3.30pm Mon, Tue, Thu & Fri, to 6pm Wed, to 1.30pm Sat

🚇 Westminster

North Transept, Sanctuary & Quire

The North Transept is often referred to as Statesmen's Aisle: politicians (notably prime ministers) and eminent public figures are commemorated by large marble statues and imposing marble plaques here. At the heart of the Abbey is the beautifully tiled sanctuary (or sacrarium), a stage for coronations, royal weddings and funerals. The Quire, a magnificent structure of gold, blue and red Victorian Gothic by Edward Blore, dates from the mid-19th century.

Lady Chapel & Chair

The spectacular Lady Chapel has a fan-vaulted ceiling, colourful heraldic banners and oak stalls. Behind the chapel's altar is the elaborate sarcophagus of Henry VII and his queen, Elizabeth of York. Opposite the entrance to the Lady Chapel is the Coronation Chair, seat of coronation for almost every monarch since the early 14th century.

Tomb of Mary Queen of Scots

There are two small chapels on either side of the Lady Chapel. On the left (north) is where Elizabeth I and her half-sister Mary I (or 'Bloody Mary') rest. On the right (south) is the tomb of Mary Queen of Scots, beheaded on the orders of her cousin Elizabeth in 1587.

Shrine of St Edward the Confessor

The most sacred spot in the abbey lies behind the high altar, where access is generally restricted to protect the 13th-century floor. St Edward was the founder of the abbey and the original building was consecrated a few weeks before his death. His tomb was slightly altered after the original was destroyed during the Reformation.

★ Top Tips

o Crowds are almost as solid as the abbey's unshakeable stonework, so get in the queue first thing in the morning.

o Join one of the 1½-hour tours led by vergers (£5 plus admission) and departing from the north door.

o Grab an audio guide, free with your entry ticket, at the north door.

✗ Take a Break

For a sit-down meal right inside the abbey head for the **Cellarium** (☏ 020-7222 0516; 20 Dean's Yard, SW1; mains £9.50-13.50; ⊙8am-6pm Mon, Tue, Thu & Fri, to 7.30pm Wed, 9am-5pm Sat, 10am-4pm Sun; 🛜), part of the original 14th-century Benedictine monastery, with stunning views of the abbey's architectural details.

Nearby, the Vincent Rooms (p59) is great for top-notch modern European cuisine at rock-bottom prices; it's operated by catering students.

Poets' Corner

The south transept contains Poets' Corner, where many of England's finest writers are buried and/or commemorated. The first poet to be buried here was Geoffrey Chaucer, joined later by Lord Alfred Tennyson, Charles Dickens, Robert Browning, Rudyard Kipling and other greats.

Sir Isaac Newton's Tomb

On the western side of the cloister is Scientists' Corner, where you will find Sir Isaac Newton's tomb. A nearby section of the northern aisle of the nave is known as Musicians' Aisle, where baroque composers Henry Purcell and John Blow are buried, as well as more modern music makers such as Benjamin Britten and Edward Elgar.

A New Abbey Museum

Scheduled for completion in 2018 are the Queen's Diamond Jubilee Galleries, a new museum and gallery space located in the medieval triforium, the arched gallery above the nave. Its exhibits will include the death masks of generations of royalty, wax effigies representing Charles II and William III (who is on a stool to make him as tall as his wife, Mary II), armour and stained glass. Highlights are the graffiti-inscribed Mary Chair and the Westminster Retable, England's oldest altarpiece, from the 13th century.

Cloisters

Providing access to the monastic buildings, the quadrangular cloisters – dating largely from the 13th to 15th centuries – would have once been a very active part of the abbey and busy with monks. The cloisters also provide access to the Chapter House, the Pyx Chamber and the Abbey Museum, situated in the vaulted undercroft.

Chapter House

The octagonal Chapter House has one of Europe's best-preserved medieval tile floors and retains traces of religious murals. Used as a meeting place by the House of Commons in the second half of the 14th century, it also boasts what is claimed to be the oldest door in the UK – it's been there 950 years.

Pyx Chamber

Next to the Chapter House and off the East Cloister, the Pyx Chamber is one of the few remaining relics of the original abbey and contains the abbey's treasures and liturgical objects. Note the enormous trunks, which were made inside the room and used to store valuables from the Exchequer.

College Garden

To reach the 900-year-old College Garden, enter Dean's Yard and the Little Cloisters off Great College St. It occupies the site of the abbey's first infirmary garden for cultivating medicinal herbs, established in the 11th century.

History of Westminster Abbey

Although a mixture of architectural styles, Westminster Abbey is considered the finest example of Early English Gothic (1190–1300). The original church was built in the 11th century by King (later St) Edward the Confessor, who is buried in the chapel behind the main altar. Henry III (r 1216–72) began work on the new building, but didn't complete it; the French Gothic nave was finished in 1388. Henry VII's huge and magnificent chapel was added in 1519.

Benedictine Monastery & Dissolution

The abbey was initially a monastery for Benedictine monks. Many of the building's features (the octagonal chapter room, the Quire and cloisters) attest to this collegial past. In 1534 Henry VIII separated the Church of England from the Catholic Church and proceeded to dissolve the country's monasteries. The King became head of the Church of England and the abbey acquired its 'royal peculiar' status (administered directly by the Crown and exempt from any ecclesiastical jurisdiction).

Site of Coronation

With the exception of Edward V and Edward VIII, every English sovereign since William the Conqueror (in 1066) has been crowned here, and most of the monarchs from Henry III (died 1272) to George II (1760) were also buried here.

Quire

The Quire, dates back to the mid-19th century. It sits where the original choir for the monks' worship would have been but bears little resemblance to the original. Nowadays, the quire is still used for singing, but its regular occupants are the Westminster Choir – 22 boys and 12 'lay vicars' (men) who sing the daily services and evensong (5pm weekdays, 3pm weekends).

Royal Wedding

On 29 April 2011 Prince William married Catherine Middleton at Westminster Abbey. The couple had chosen the abbey for the relatively intimate setting of the Sanctuary – because of the Quire, three-quarters of the 1900-or-so guests couldn't see a thing!

Top Sight 📷
Buckingham Palace

Built in 1705 for the Duke of Buckingham and then purchased by George III, the palace has been the Royal Family's London lodgings since 1837 when Queen Victoria moved in. Commoners can now get a peek of the State Rooms, a mere 19 of the palace's 775 rooms, from late July to September when HRH (Her Royal Highness) takes her holidays in Scotland.

◎ MAP P54, A4

www.royalcollection.org.uk

Buckingham Palace Rd, SW1

adult/child/under 5yr £24/13.50/free

⏱9.30am-7pm (to 6pm Sep) Jul-Sep only

⊖ Green Park, St James's Park

State Rooms

The tour starts in the Grand Hall at the foot of the monumental Grand Staircase, takes in John Nash's Italianate Green Drawing Room, the State Dining Room, the Blue Drawing Room (which has a gorgeous fluted ceiling by Nash) and the White Drawing Room, where foreign ambassadors are received. The Throne Room is rather anticlimactic, with his-and-her pink chairs monogrammed 'ER' and 'P'.

Picture Gallery & Gardens

The 47m-long Picture Gallery features splendid works by such artists as Van Dyck, Rembrandt, Canaletto, Poussin, Rubens, Canova and Vermeer. Wandering the 18 hectares of gardens at the end of the tour is another highlight – as well as admiring some of the 350 or so species of flowers and plants.

Queen's Gallery

The Royal Family has amassed a priceless collection of paintings, sculpture, ceramics, furniture and jewellery. The splendid **Queen's Gallery** (South Wing, Buckingham Palace; adult/child £10.30/5.30, incl Royal Mews £19/10; ⊙10am-5.30pm) showcases some of the palace's treasures on a rotating basis. Entrance to the gallery is from Buckingham Gate.

Royal Mews

Southwest of the palace, the **Royal Mews** (Buckingham Palace Rd; adult/child £11/6.40, incl Queen's Gallery £19/10; ⊙10am-5pm Apr-Oct, to 4pm Mon-Sat Feb, Mar & Nov; ⊖Victoria) started life as a falconry but is now a working stable looking after the royals' immaculately groomed horses, along with the opulent vehicles the monarch uses for transport. Highlights include the magnificent Gold State Coach of 1762, and the 1911 Glass Coach.

★ Top Tips

o Entry to the palace is by timed ticket (departures every quarter-hour) which must be booked online. The self-guided tour (audio guide included) takes about two hours.

o A Royal Day Out (adult/child/under 5yr £39.50/22/free) is a combined ticket including entry to the State Rooms, Queen's Gallery and Royal Mews.

o The Changing of the Guard (p56) is very popular; arrive early to secure a good view.

✕ Take a Break

A pleasant place for a snack after visiting the palace or viewing the Changing of the Guard is **St James's Cafe** (☏ 020-7839 1149; St James's Park, SW1; mains £6.50-11; ⊙8am-6pm Mon-Sat, 9am-5pm Sun, to 10pm Apr-Oct; ☎; ⊖Charing Cross, St James's Park).

For an Indian repast fit for a maharajah, head for nearby Quilon (p60), which boasts a Michelin star.

Top Sight 📷
Houses of Parliament

Both the elected House of Commons and the House of Lords, who are appointed or hereditary, sit in the sumptuous Palace of Westminster, a neo-Gothic confection dating from the mid-19th century (with a few sections that survived a catastrophic fire in 1834). A visit here is a journey to the very heart of British democracy.

◉ MAP P54, F5

Palace of Westminster
www.parliament.uk
Parliament Sq, SW1
admission free
⊖ Westminster

Big Ben

The most famous feature of the Houses of Parliament is the Clock Tower, officially named the Elizabeth Tower to mark the Queen's Diamond Jubilee in 2012 but commonly known as Big Ben. Big Ben is actually the 13.5-tonne bell hanging inside and is named after Benjamin Hall, the first Commissioner of Works when the tower was completed in 1858.

Westminster Hall

One of the most interesting features of the Palace of Westminster, seat of the English monarchy from the 11th to the early 16th centuries, is Westminster Hall. Originally built at the end of the 11th century, it is the oldest surviving part of the complex; the awesome hammer-beam roof was added between 1394 and 1401.

House of Commons

The House of Commons is where Members of Parliament (MPs) meet to propose and discuss new legislation and to grill the prime minister and other ministers. The chamber, designed by Giles Gilbert Scott, replaced the one destroyed by a 1941 bomb.

House of Lords

The House of Lords is visited via the amusingly named Strangers' Gallery. The intricate 'Tudor Gothic' interior led its architect, Auguste Pugin (1812–52), to an early death from overwork and nervous strain.

Tours

Visitors are welcome on either self-guided or **guided tours** (adult/child £28/12) on Saturdays year-round and on most weekdays during parliamentary recesses.

★ Top Tips

○ To find out what's being debated on a particular day, check the notice board beside the entrance, or check online at www.parliament.uk.

○ UK residents can approach their MPs to arrange a free tour and to climb the Elizabeth Tower.

○ Afternoon tea (£29) in the Terrace Pavilion overlooking the River Thames is a popular add-on to the tours.

✕ Take a Break

The brick-vaulted **Footstool** (2-/3-course set lunch £17.50/19.50; ⊙8.30am-5pm Mon-Fri, 2hr before St John's concert performances Sat & Sun; ⊙St James's Park, Westminster), a cafe and restaurant in the crypt of St John's, Smith Square, is a short walk south of the Palace.

If you're continuing your tour on the South Bank, consider having lunch in the elegant Skylon (p140) in the Royal Festival Hall.

Walking Tour 🥾

Royal London

Lassoing the cream of London's royal and stately sights, this attraction-packed walk ticks off some of the city's truly must-do experiences on one comprehensive route. You'll be passing some of London's most famous buildings and historic sites, so photo opportunities abound. The walk conveniently returns you in a loop to your starting point for easy access to other parts of London.

Walk Facts

Start Westminster Abbey;
⊖ Westminster

End Houses of Parliament;
⊖ Westminster

Length 3.5km; two hours

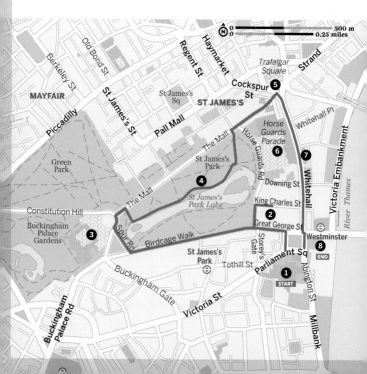

❶ Westminster Abbey

Start by exploring mighty Westminster Abbey (p44), preferably early (before the crowds arrive). This is where almost every English sovereign since 1066 has been crowned.

❷ Churchill War Rooms

Walk around Parliament Sq, past the UK Supreme Court (it's free to sit in courtrooms during hearings) on the west side of the square, to the Churchill War Rooms (p56) to discover how Churchill coordinated the Allied war against Hitler.

❸ Buckingham Palace

Walking to the end of Birdcage Walk brings you to majestic Buckingham Palace (p48), where the state rooms are accessible to ticket holders in August and September. Alternatively, pay a visit to the Royal Mews (p49) and the Queen's Gallery (p49), both nearby.

❹ St James's Park

Amble along The Mall and enter St James's Park (p57), one of London's most attractive royal parks. Walk alongside St James's Park Lake for its plentiful ducks, geese, swans and other waterfowl.

❺ Trafalgar Square

Return to The Mall and pass through Admiralty Arch to Trafalgar Sq for regal views down to the Houses of Parliament.

❻ Horse Guards Parade

Walk down Whitehall to the entrance to Horse Guards Parade (p58). The dashing mounted sentries of the Queen's Household Cavalry are on duty here daily from 10am to 4pm, when the dismounted guards are changed.

❼ Banqueting House

On the far side of the street, magnificent Banqueting House (p58) is the last surviving remnant of Whitehall Palace, which once stretched most of the way down Whitehall but vanished in a late-17th-century fire. Further down Whitehall is the entrance to No 10 Downing Street.

❽ Houses of Parliament

At the end of Whitehall, you'll reach the magnificently Gothic Houses of Parliament (p50) and its famous tower, Big Ben. You can tour the building and even sit during the debate.

✕ Take a Break

Pack a picnic to eat in lovely **St James's Park** if it's a sunny day. Alternatively, **Cafe Murano** (p60) in the nearby neighbourhood of St James's is a fine choice for authentic and delicious cuisine from northern Italy.

Westminster Abbey & Westminster

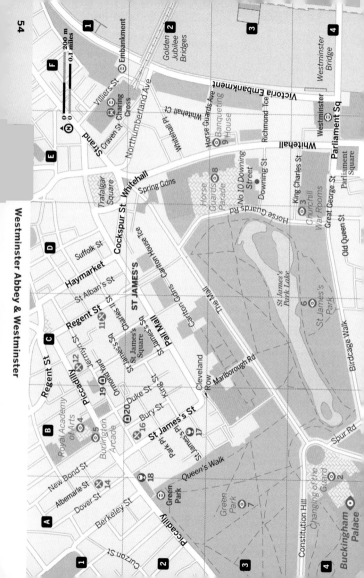

200 m
0.1 miles

F
Embankment ⊖
Charing Cross ⊖
Villiers St
Craven St
Strand
Northumberland Ave
Golden Jubilee Bridges **2**

E
Trafalgar Square
Whitehall
Spring Gdns
Whitehall PI
Whitehall Ct
Horse Guards Ave
Banqueting House ⊙ 9
Victoria Embankment
Richmond Tce
3
Westminster Bridge
Parliament Sq
Westminster ⊖

D
Suffolk St
Haymarket
St Alban's St
Cockspur St
Whitehall
Horse Guards Parade
⊙ 8
Horse Guards Rd
No 10 Downing Street
Downing St
Churchill War Rooms ⊙ 3
King Charles St
Great George St
Parliament Square
Old Queen St

C
Regent St
ST JAMES'S
Regent St ✕ 11
St James's St
Charles II St
St James's Square
St James's Sq
Pall Mall
Carlton Gdns
Carlton House Tce
The Mall
St James's Park Lake
St James's Park
⊙ 6
Birdcage Walk

B
Royal Academy of Arts
⊙ 4
⊙ 5
Burlington Arcade
Piccadilly ⊖
✕ 12
Jermyn St
Ormond Yard
19 ⊙
✕ 20
Duke St
King St
Bury St
St James's St
16 ✕
St James's Sq
17 ⊙
Cleveland Row
Marlborough Rd
Spur Rd
Queen's Walk
Changing of the Guard
⊙ 2
Buckingham Palace

A
New Bond St
Albemarle St
✕ 14
Dover St
Berkeley St
Piccadilly
⊙ 18
Green Park ⊖
Green Park
⊙ 7
Constitution Hill
Curzon St

1 **2** **3** **4**

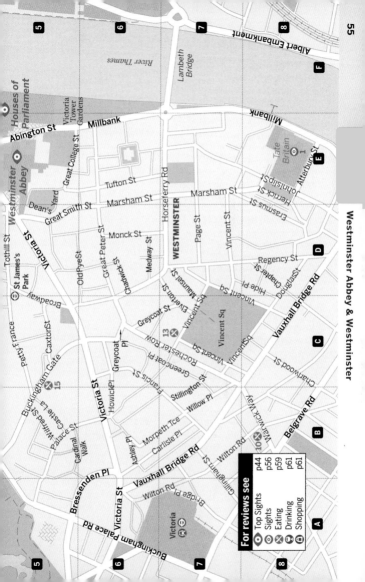

Sights

Tate Britain

GALLERY

1 MAP P54, E8

The older and more venerable of the two Tate siblings celebrates British works from 1500 to the present, including those from Blake, Hogarth, Gainsborough, Barbara Hepworth, Whistler, Constable and Turner, as well as vibrant modern and contemporary pieces from Lucian Freud, Francis Bacon and Henry Moore. Join a free 45-minute **thematic tour** (11am, noon, 2pm & 3pm daily) and 15-minute **Art in Focus** (1.15pm Tue, Thu & Sat) talks. (020-7887 8888; www.tate.org.uk/visit/tate-britain; Millbank, SW1; admission free; 10am-6pm, to 9.30pm on selected Fri; Pimlico)

Changing of the Guard

CEREMONY

2 MAP P54, B4

A London 'must see', this is when the Old Guard (Foot Guards of the Household Regiment) comes off duty to be replaced by the New Guard on the forecourt of Buckingham Palace (p48). Tourists gape – sometimes from behind as many as 10 people – at the bright-red uniforms, bearskin hats and full-on pageantry. The official name for the ceremony is Guard Mounting and it lasts for around 45 minutes. (http://changing-guard.com; Buckingham Palace, Buckingham Palace Rd, SW1; St James's Park, Victoria, Green Park)

Churchill War Rooms

MUSEUM

3 MAP P54, D4

Winston Churchill helped coordinate the Allied resistance against Nazi Germany on a Bakelite telephone from this underground complex during WWII. The **Cabinet War Rooms** remain much as they were when the lights were switched off in 1945, capturing the drama and dogged spirit of the time, while the multimedia **Churchill Museum** affords intriguing insights into the life and times of the resolute, cigar-smoking wartime leader. (www.iwm.org.uk/visits/churchill-war-rooms; Clive Steps, King Charles St, SW1; adult/child £21/10.50; 9.30am-6pm; Westminster)

Royal Academy of Arts

GALLERY

4 MAP P54, B1

Britain's oldest society devoted to fine arts was founded in 1768 and moved to Burlington House exactly a century later. The collection contains drawings, paintings, architectural designs, photographs and sculptures by past and present academicians, such as Joshua Reynolds, John Constable, Thomas Gainsborough, JMW Turner, David Hockney and Norman Foster. (020-7300 8000; www.royalacademy.org.uk; Burlington House, Piccadilly, W1; adult/child from £13.50/free, exhibition prices vary; 10am-6pm Sat-Thu, to 10pm Fri; Green Park)

Burlington Arcade

HISTORIC BUILDING

5 ◉ MAP P54, B1

Flanking Burlington House, which is home to the Royal Academy of Arts, is this delightful arcade, built in 1819. Today it is a shopping precinct for the wealthy, and is most famous for the Burlington Beadles, uniformed guards who patrol the area keeping an eye out for such offences as running, chewing gum, whistling, opening umbrellas or anything else that could lower the tone. (The fact that the arcade once served as a brothel is kept quiet.)

Running perpendicular to it between Old Bond and Albermarle Sts is the more recent 1880 **Royal Arcade** (btwn 28 Old Bond & 12 Albe-marle Sts, W1; ◉ Green Park). (www.burlington-arcade.co.uk; 51 Piccadilly, W1; ⏱ 9am-7.30pm Mon-Sat, 11am-6pm Sun; ◉ Green Park)

St James's Park

PARK

6 ◉ MAP P54, C4

At just 23 hectares, St James's is the second smallest of the eight royal parks after Green Park (p58). But what it lacks in size it makes up for in grooming as it is the most manicured green space in London. It has brilliant views of the London Eye, Westminster, St James's Palace, Carlton Tce and the Horse Guards Parade; the photo-perfect sight of Buckingham Palace from the footbridge spanning the central lake is the best you'll find. (www.royalparks.org.uk/parks/st-jamess-park; The Mall,

Buckingham Palace (p48) and St James's Park

SW1; ⊘5am-midnight; ⊖St James's Park, Green Park)

Green Park PARK

7 ⊙ MAP P54, A3

At 19 hectares Green Park is the smallest of the eight royal parks. Still, it has huge plane and oak trees and undulating meadows, and it's never as crowded as its neighbour, the more manicured St James's Park (p57). It was once a duelling ground and, like Hyde Park (p158), served as a vegetable garden during WWII.

It famously has no flower beds as they were banned by Queen Catherine of Braganza after she learned her philandering husband Charles II had been picking posies for his mistresses. Or so the story goes... (www.royalparks.org.uk/parks/green-park; ⊘5am-midnight; ⊖Green Park)

Horse Guards Parade HISTORIC SITE

8 ⊙ MAP P54, E3

In a more accessible version of Buckingham Palace's Changing of the Guard (p56), the mounted troops of the Household Cavalry's two regiments, the Life Guards and the Blues & Royals, change guard here daily at 11am (10am Sunday), at what is the official vehicular entrance to the royal palaces. A slightly less ceremonial version takes place at 4pm when the dismounted guards are changed. On the

Queen's official birthday in June, the **Trooping the Colour** (www. trooping-the-colour.co.uk; ⊘Jun) takes place here.

During the reigns of Henry VIII and his daughter Elizabeth I, jousting tournaments were staged here. The parade ground and its buildings were built in 1745 to house the Queen's so-called Life Guards. Here you'll also find the **Household Cavalry Museum** (📞020-7930 3070; adult/child £7/5; ⊘10am-6pm Apr-Oct, to 5pm Nov-Mar). (http://changing-guard.com/queens-life-guard.html; ⊘11am Mon-Sat, 10am Sun; ⊖Westminster, Charing Cross, Embankment)

Banqueting House PALACE

9 ⊙ MAP P54, E3

Banqueting House is the sole surviving section of the Tudor Whitehall Palace (1532) that once stretched most of the way down Whitehall before burning to the ground in a 1698 conflagration. Designed by Inigo Jones in 1622 and refaced in Portland stone in the 19th century, Banqueting House was England's first purely Renaissance building and resembled no other structure in the country at the time. The English apparently loathed it for over a century. (📞020-3166 6000; www.hrp.org.uk/banquetinghouse; Whitehall, SW1; adult/child £6.50/free; ⊘10am-5pm; ⊖Westminster)

No 10 Downing St

The official office of British leaders since 1732, when George II presented No 10 to 'First Lord of the Treasury' Robert Walpole, **No 10 Downing St** (Map p54, E3; www.number10.gov.uk; 10 Downing St, SW1; ⊖Westminster) has also been the prime minister's London residence since refurbishment in 1902. For such a famous address, No 10 is a small-looking Georgian building on a plain-looking street, hardly warranting comparison with the White House, for example. Yet it is actually three houses joined into one and boasts roughly 100 rooms plus a 2000-sq-metre garden.

Eating

Pimlico Fresh   CAFE £

10 ⊗ MAP P54, B8

This friendly two-room cafe will see you right whether you need breakfast (French toast, bowls of porridge laced with honey or maple syrup), lunch (homemade quiches and soups, 'things' on toast) or just a good old latte and cake. (⟟020-7932 0030; 86 Wilton Rd, SW1; mains from £4.50; ⊙7.30am-7.30pm Mon-Fri, 9am-6pm Sat & Sun; ⊖Victoria)

Shoryu   NOODLES £

11 ⊗ MAP P54, C1

Compact, well-mannered and central noodle-parlour Shoryu draws in reams of noodle diners to feast at its wooden counters and small tables. It's busy, friendly and efficient, with helpful and informative staff. Fantastic *tonkotsu* pork-broth ramen is the name of the game here, sprinkled with *nori* (dried, pressed seaweed), spring onion, *nitamago* (soft-boiled eggs)

and sesame seeds. No bookings. (www.shoryuramen.com; 9 Regent St, SW1; mains £10-14.50; ⊙11.15am-midnight Mon-Sat, to 10.30pm Sun; ⊖Piccadilly Circus)

Kahve Dünyası   CAFE £

12 ⊗ MAP P54, C1

As lovers of all things Turkic, we were (and remain) over the moon that a branch of our favourite Turkish cafe chain has opened in central London, with pistachio-based desserts, real *lokum* (Turkish delight) and mastic ice cream. Oh, and Turkish coffee – the best in the world. Stunning service. Eat-off-the-floor clean. (Coffee World; ⟟020-7287 9063; http://kahvedunyasi.co.uk; Unit 3, 200 Piccadilly, W1; cakes £3.85-4.95; ⊙7.30am-10pm Mon-Fri, to 10.30pm Sat, to 9.30pm Sun; ⊖Piccadilly)

Vincent Rooms   MODERN EUROPEAN £

13 ⊗ MAP P54, C7

Care to be a guinea pig for student chefs at Westminster Kingsway

Westminster Nightlife?

Westminster and Whitehall are totally deserted in the evenings, with little in the way of bars or restaurants. It's pretty much the same story for St James's. If you find yourself in Westminster in the early evening, head north to vibrant Soho for fantastic bars and restaurants, or to the lively streets surrounding Covent Garden.

College, where such celebrity chefs as Jamie Oliver and Ainsley Harriott were trained? Service is eager to please, the atmosphere in both the Brasserie and the Escoffier Room smarter than expected, and the food (including veggie options) ranges from wonderful to exquisite – at very affordable prices. (☏020-7802 8391; www.westking.ac.uk/about-us/vincent-rooms-restaurant; Westminster Kingsway College, Vincent Sq, SW1; mains £9-13; ⏱noon-3pm Mon-Fri, 6-9pm Tue-Thu; ⊖Victoria)

Gymkhana   INDIAN ££

14 ⊗ MAP P54, A1

The rather sombre setting is all British Raj: ceiling fans, oak ceiling, period cricket photos and hunting trophies, but the menu is lively, bright and inspiring. For lovers of variety, there is a six-course tasting meat/vegetarian menu (£70/65). The bar is open to 1am.

(☏020-3011 5900; www.gym-khanalondon.com; 42 Albemarle St, W1; mains £10-38, 4-course lunch/dinner £28.50/40; ⏱noon-2.30pm & 5.30-10.15pm Mon-Sat; 🛜; ⊖Green Park)

Quilon   INDIAN £££

15 ⊗ MAP P54, C5

This award-winning, Michelin-starred restaurant probably serves the best and most inventive Indian food in London. While the restaurant itself in posh St James's is nothing to write home about, the dishes themselves demand not postcards but missives: pink pepper chilli prawns, Malabar lamb biryani, stuffed quail legs. The menu is very vegetarian friendly, with up to a dozen unique choices. (☏020-7821 1899; www.quilon.co.uk; 41 Buckingham Gate, SW1; mains £18-35; ⏱noon-2.30pm & 6-11pm Mon-Fri, 12.30-3.30pm & 6-11pm Sat, 12.30-3.30pm & 6-10.30pm Sun; ⊖St James's Park)

Cafe Murano   ITALIAN ££

16 ⊗ MAP P54, B2

The setting may seem somewhat demure at this superb and busy restaurant, but with such a sublime North Italian menu on offer, it sees no need to be flashy and of-the-moment. You get what you come for, and the lobster linguini, pork belly and cod with mussels and samphire are as close to culinary perfection as you'll get. (☏020-3371 5559; www.cafemurano.co.uk; 33 St James's St, SW1; mains £18-25, 2-/3-course set meal £19/23;

⏱noon-3pm & 5.30-11pm Mon-Sat, 11.30am-4pm Sun; ❸Green Park)

Drinking

Dukes London COCKTAIL BAR

17 🚇 MAP P54, B2

Sip to-die-for Martinis like royalty in a gentleman's-club-like ambience at this tucked-away classic bar where white-jacketed masters mix up some awesomely good preparations. Ian Fleming used to frequent the place, perhaps perfecting his 'shaken, not stirred' James Bond maxim. Smokers can ease into the secluded Cognac and Cigar Garden to light up cigars purchased here. (📞020-7491 4840; www.dukeshotel.com/dukes-bar; Dukes Hotel, 35 St James's Pl, SW1; ⏱2-11pm Mon-Sat, 4-10.30pm Sun; 📶; ❸Green Park)

Rivoli Bar COCKTAIL BAR

18 🚇 MAP P54, B2

You may not quite need a diamond as big as the Ritz to drink at this art deco marvel, but it might help. All camphor wood, illuminated Lalique glass, golden ceiling domes and stunning cocktails, the bar is a gem. Unlike in some other parts of the Ritz, dress code here is smart casual. (📞020-7300 2340; www.theritzlondon.com/rivoli-bar; Ritz London, 150 Piccadilly, W1; ⏱11.30am-11.30pm Mon-Sat, noon-10.30pm Sun; 📶; ❸Green Park)

Shopping

Paxton & Whitfield FOOD & DRINKS

19 🔒 MAP P54, C1

With modest beginnings as an Aldwych stall in 1742 and purveying a dizzying range of fine cheeses, this black- and gold-fronted shop holds two royal warrants. Whatever your cheese leanings, you'll find the shop well supplied with hard and soft cheeses as well as blue and washed-rind examples. (📞020-7930 0259; www.paxtonandwhitfield.co.uk; 93 Jermyn St, W1; ⏱10am-6.30pm Mon-Sat, 11am-5pm Sun; ❸Piccadilly Circus, Green Park)

Taylor of Old Bond Street COSMETICS

20 🔒 MAP P54, B2

Plying its trade since the mid-19th century, this shop supplies the 'well-groomed gentleman' with every sort of razor, shaving brush and scent of shaving soap imaginable – not to mention oils, soaps and other bath products. (📞020-7930 5321; www.tayloroldbondst.co.uk; 74 Jermyn St, SW1; ⏱8.30am-6pm Mon-Sat; ❸Green Park, Piccadilly Circus)

Walking Tour 🥾

Tower of London to the Tate Modern

Commencing at one of London's most historic sights, this walk crosses the Thames on magnificent Tower Bridge, before heading west along the river, scooping up some excellent views and passing breathtaking modern architecture, history and Shakespeare's Globe on the way. It comes to a halt amid the renowned artworks of the Tate Modern.

Walk Facts

Start Tower of London;
🚇 Tower Hill

End Tate Modern;
🚇 Blackfriars

Length 3km; 1½ hours

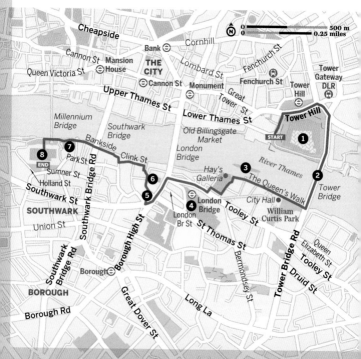

1 Tower of London

Rising commandingly over the Thames, the ancient Tower of London (p112) enjoys a dramatic location. Be dazzled by the vast Koh-i-Noor diamond, explore the impressive White Tower and tag along with a Yeoman Warder on an enlightening tour.

2 Tower Bridge

Cross ornate 19th-century Tower Bridge – traversed by more than 40,000 people daily – to the south side of the Thames.

3 HMS Belfast

Walk west along Queen's Walk past **City Hall** (⏱8.30am-5.30pm Mon-Fri), called the 'Leaning Tower of Pizzas' by some. Moored a bit further ahead, HMS Belfast (p138), a light cruiser that served in WWII and later conflicts, is a floating museum.

4 Shard

Pop through the shopping complex of Hay's Galleria to Tooley St to see the **Shard** (p139), designed by Italian architect Renzo Piano. Views from the tallest building in the European Union are breathtaking, but come at a price.

5 Borough Market

Keep walking west along Tooley St and dip down Borough High St to head up Stoney St to Borough Market (p136), overflowing with tasty produce from Thursday

to Saturday. If you fancy a beer, keep walking along Stoney St to the **Rake** (📞020-7407 0557; www.utobeer.co.uk; 14 Winchester Walk, SE1; ⏱noon-11pm Mon-Fri, 11am-11pm Sat, noon-10pm Sun; 🚇London Bridge) on Winchester Walk.

6 Southwark Cathedral

Southwark Cathedral (p137) is both fascinating and relaxing. Parts of the church date to medieval times and its treasured haul of artefacts includes a lovely Elizabethan sideboard and an icon of Jesus.

7 Shakespeare's Globe

Wander west along Clink St – and past the remains of Winchester Palace – to Bankside and on to Shakespeare's Globe (p136). Join one of the tours if you have time.

8 Tate Modern

Not far west of Shakespeare's Globe is the Millennium Bridge (p138) and London's standout modern and contemporary-art gallery, the Tate Modern (p130).

✕ Take a Break

On Friday and Saturday, grab takeaway from one of the many stalls at **Borough Market**. On other days head to **Arabica Bar & Kitchen** (p142) for wonderful contemporary Middle Eastern cuisine.

Explore ⊕
National Gallery & Covent Garden

At the centre of the West End – London's physical, cultural and social heart – the neighbourhood around the National Gallery and Covent Garden is a sightseeing hub. This is London's busiest neighbourhood, with a grand convergence of monumental history, stylish restaurants, standout entertainment choices and classic pubs. And if you're in town to shop, you'll be in heaven.

Start with the National Gallery (p66). Trafalgar Sq (p72) is perfect for a break and sublime views, and the nearby National Portrait Gallery (p72) has some outstanding exhibits. Lunch can be expediently supplied by its splendid Portrait (p78) restaurant. Walk off your meal, heading east along the Strand to browse around Covent Garden Piazza (p74), shopping, exploring and watching the street performers. The London Transport Museum (p73) is excellent, especially if you're with kids. Take the lift up to 5th View (p76) on Piccadilly, or get in line for tapas at Barrafina (p76). If post-dinner drinks are in order, make it the Lamb & Flag (p80) or Gordon's Wine Bar (p80); otherwise buy tickets for a West End musical, theatre performance or opera to round out the night.

Getting There & Around

⊖ Piccadilly Circus, Leicester Sq and Covent Garden (all Piccadilly Line), or Leicester Sq, Charing Cross and Embankment (all Northern Line).

Covent Garden Map on p70

Trafalgar Square (p72) ALICE-PHOTO/SHUTTERSTOCK ©

Top Sight 📷

National Gallery

With some 2300 European paintings on display, this is one of the world's richest art collections, with seminal paintings from the mid-13th to the early 20th century, including works by Leonardo da Vinci, Michelangelo, Titian, Van Gogh and Renoir.

◉ MAP P70, E6

📞 020-7747 2885

www.nationalgallery.org.uk

Trafalgar Sq, WC2

admission free

🕘 10am-6pm Sat-Thu, to 9pm Fri

🚇 Charing Cross

Sainsbury Wing

The Sainsbury Wing (1260–1510) houses plenty of fine religious paintings commissioned for private devotion, as well as more unusual masterpieces such as Botticelli's *Venus & Mars*. Leonardo Da Vinci's *Virgin of the Rocks* (room 66) is a visual and technical masterpiece.

West & North Wings

Works from the High Renaissance (1500–1600) embellish the West Wing where Michelangelo, Titian, Raphael, Correggio, El Greco and Bronzino hold court; Rubens, Rembrandt and Caravaggio grace the North Wing (1600–1700). Notable here are two self-portraits of Rembrandt (at age 34 in room 24 and at 63 in room 23) and the beautiful *Rokeby Venus* by Velázquez in room 30.

East Wing

The East Wing (1700–1900) has works by 18th-century British artists such as Gainsborough, Constable and Turner, and seminal Impressionist and post-Impressionist masterpieces by Van Gogh, Renoir and Monet await.

Rain, Steam & Speed: The Great Western Railway

In Room 34, this magnificent oil painting from Turner was created in 1844. Generally considered to depict the Maidenhead Railway Bridge, the painting reveals the forces reshaping the world at the time: railways, speed and a reinterpretation of the use of light, atmosphere and colour in art. Look for the dashing hare.

Sunflowers

In Room 45 hangs one of several sunflower still lifes painted by Van Gogh in late 1888; this masterpiece displays a variety of then-innovative artistic techniques, while the vividness of the colour convey a powerful sense of affirmation.

★ Top Tips

o Free one-hour introductory guided tours leave from the information desk in the Sainsbury Wing daily at 11.30am and 2.30pm, and at 7pm on Friday.

o If you want to go it alone, the comprehensive audio guide (£4) is highly recommended.

o There are also special trails and activity sheets for children.

o The National Gallery is open till 9pm on Friday.

✕ Take a Break

The **National Dining Rooms** (⊘10am-5.30pm Sat-Thu, to 8.30pm Fri; mains £14.50-21), anchor restaurant at the gallery, offers a filling but pricey County Menu that changes monthly.

Also here is the **National Cafe** (⊘8am-7pm Mon, to 10pm Tue-Thu, to 10.30pm Fri, 9am-7pm Sat, 9am-6pm Sun; 2-/3-course set lunch £17/21) which has light meals and a proper sit-down bistro.

Walking Tour 🚶‍♀️

A Stroll Through Soho

Soho may come into its own in the evenings, but daytime guarantees other surprises and opportunities to be charmed by the area's bohemian and bookish leanings, vitality, diversity, architecture narratives and creative energy. Thread your way from Chinatown through intriguing backstreets, genteel squares and street markets to one of the neighbourhood's signature bars.

Walk Facts

Start Chinatown;
🚇 Leicester Sq

End French Hose Soho;
🚇 Leicester Sq or
Piccadilly Circus

Length 2km; three to
six hours

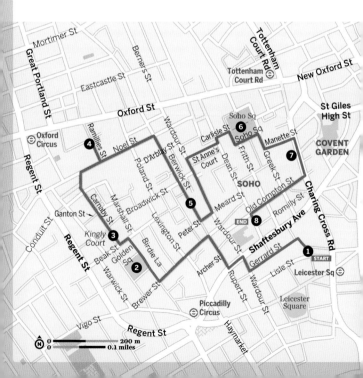

1 Explore Chinatown

Just north of Leicester Sq tube station are Lisle and Gerrard Sts, a focal point for London's Chinese community. A tight tangle of supermarkets, roast-duck shops and dim sum canteens,

2 Relax in Golden Square

North of Brewer St, historic Golden Sq – featured in Charles Dickens' *The Life and Adventures of Nicholas Nickleby* – was once part of an area called Windmill Fields. This lovely 17th-century square was in all probability Christopher Wren's design. The garden in the middle is a relaxing place to find a bench.

3 Designer Shopping on Carnaby Street

With its pretty, colourful facades, pedestrian Carnaby St (and streets like Great Marlborough St fanning off it) is a haven for brands and designer boutiques. All the big names – from MAC to Miss Sixty, Levi's to the North Face – have shops here and the crowds never seem to thin.

4 Visit the Photographers' Gallery

The fantastic **Photographers' Gallery** (16-18 Ramillies St, W1; adult/child £4/free; ⏱10am-6pm Mon-Sat, to 8pm Thu, 11am-6pm Sun) has five floors of exhibition space, a cafe and a shop brimming with prints and photography books. It has awarded the prestigious Deutsche Börse Photography Prize annually since 1997.

5 Pick up Picnic Supplies in Berwick Street Market

Berwick Street Market (⏱9am-6pm Mon-Sat) has been here since the late 18th century and is a great place to put together a picnic, or shop for a prepared meal. Berwick St is famously the location of the Oasis album cover *(What's the Story) Morning Glory?*

6 Stopover in Soho Square

Cut through tiny St Anne's Ct to Dean St (where Karl Marx and family lived at No 28 between 1851–56). Leafy Soho Sq beyond is where people come to laze in the sun on warm days. Laid out in 1681, it was originally named King's Sq.

7 Browse Foyles

Even the most obscure titles await discovery at **Foyles** (⏱9.30am-9pm Mon-Sat, 11.30am-6pm Sun), London's legendary bookshop. **Grant & Cutler** (⏱9.30am-9pm Mon-Sat, 11.30am-6pm Sun), the UK's largest foreign-language bookseller, is on the 4th floor; the lovely cafe on the 5th.

8 Quaff Wine in French House

Walk down Old Compton St to Soho's legendary boho boozer, **French House Soho** (⏱noon-11pm Mon-Sat, to 10.30pm Sun), the meeting place of Free French Forces during WWII – de Gaulle is said to have drunk here often, while Dylan Thomas, Peter O'Toole and Francis Bacon frequently ended up horizontal.

N

0   200 m
0   0.1 miles

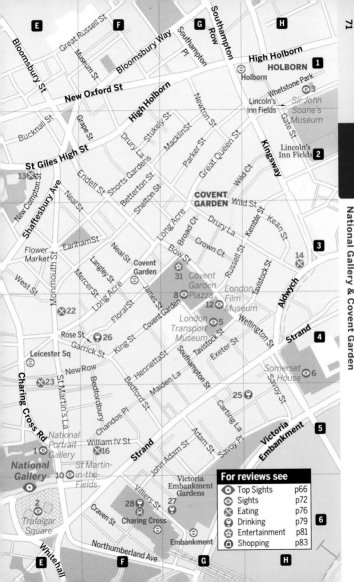

Sights

National Portrait Gallery

GALLERY

1 ⊙ MAP P70, E5

What makes the National Portrait Gallery so compelling is its familiarity; in many cases, you'll have heard of the subject (royals, scientists, politicians, celebrities) or the artist (Andy Warhol, Annie Leibovitz, Lucian Freud) but not necessarily recognise the face. Highlights include the famous 'Chandos portrait' of William Shakespeare, the first artwork the gallery acquired (in 1856) and believed to be the only likeness made during the playwright's lifetime, and a touching sketch of novelist Jane Austen by her sister. (☏020-7321 0055; www.npg.org.uk; St Martin's Pl, WC2; admission free; ⊙10am-6pm Sat-Wed, to 9pm Thu & Fri; ⊖Charing Cross, Leicester Sq)

Trafalgar Square

SQUARE

2 ⊙ MAP P70, E6

Trafalgar Sq is the true centre of London, where rallies and marches take place, tens of thousands of revellers usher in the New Year and locals congregate for anything from communal open-air cinema and Christmas celebrations to political protests. It is dominated by the 52m-high **Nelson's Column** and ringed by many splendid buildings, including the National Gallery (p66) and the church of St Martin-in-the-Fields (p74). (⊖Charing Cross)

Sir John Soane's Museum

MUSEUM

3 ⊙ MAP P70, H1

This little museum is one of the most atmospheric and fascinating in London. The building was the beautiful, bewitching home of architect Sir John Soane (1753–1837), which he left brimming with his vast architectural and archaeological collection, as well as intriguing personal effects and curiosities. The museum represents his exquisite and eccentric tastes, persuasions and proclivities. (☏020-7405 2107; www.soane.org; 12 Lincoln's Inn Fields, WC2; admission free; ⊙10am-5pm Wed-Sun; ⊖Holborn)

St James's Piccadilly

CHURCH

4 ⊙ MAP P70, B6

The only church (1684) Christopher Wren built from scratch and one of a handful established on a new site (most of the other London churches are replacements for those destroyed in the Great Fire), this simple building substitutes what some might call the pompous flourishes of Wren's most famous churches with a warm and elegant accessibility. The baptismal font portraying Adam and Eve on the shaft and the altar reredos are by Grinling Gibbons. (☏020-7734 4511; www.sjp.org.uk; 197 Piccadilly, W1; ⊙8am-8pm; ⊖Piccadilly Circus)

Fourth Plinth Project

Three of the four plinths at Trafalgar Sq's corners are occupied by notables: King George IV on horseback, and military men General Sir Charles Napier and Major General Sir Henry Havelock. The other, originally intended for a statue of William IV, remained largely vacant for more than a century and a half. The Royal Society of Arts conceived what is now called the Fourth Plinth Commission in 1999, deciding to use the empty space for works by contemporary artists. Works exhibited for 18 months in 'the smallest sculpture park in the world' are invariably both fun and challenging, creating a sense of dissonance with the grand surrounds of Trafalgar Sq.

London Transport Museum   MUSEUM

5 ⊙ MAP P70, G4

This entertaining and informative museum looks at how London developed as a result of better transport and contains horse-drawn omnibuses, early taxis, underground trains you can drive yourself, a detailed look at Crossrail (a new high-frequency 75-mile rail service linking Reading with Essex), and everything in between, including signage. Start on Level 2 and don't miss the museum shop for imaginative souvenirs, including historical tube posters, 'Mind the Gap' socks and 'Way Out' T-shirts. (☑020-7379 6344; www.ltmuseum.co.uk; Covent Garden Piazza, WC2; adult/child £17.50/free; ⊙10am-6pm; ⊖Covent Garden)

Somerset House   HISTORIC BUILDING

6 ⊙ MAP P70, H4

Designed by William Chambers in 1775 for government departments

and royal societies – in fact, the world's first office block – Somerset House now contains several fabulous galleries. In the North Wing near the Strand entrance, the **Courtauld Gallery** (http://courtauld.ac.uk; adult/child £8/free, temporary exhibitions vary; ⊙10am-6pm) displays a wealth of 14th- to 20th-century art, including masterpieces by Rubens, Botticelli, Cézanne, Degas, Renoir, Seurat, Manet, Monet, Leger and others. The **Embankment Galleries** in the South Wing are devoted to temporary (mostly photographic, design and fashion) exhibitions; prices and hours vary. (☑020-7845 4600; www.somersethouse.org.uk; The Strand, WC2; ⊙galleries 10am-6pm, courtyard 7.30am-11pm, terrace 8am-11pm; ⊖Temple, Covent Garden)

Piccadilly Circus   SQUARE

7 ⊙ MAP P70, C5

Architect John Nash had originally designed Regent St and Piccadilly in the 1820s to be the two most

Fun at Somerset House

The courtyard of Somerset House (p73) is transformed into a popular ice-skating rink in winter and used for concerts and events in summer. The **Summer Screen** (when the Great Court turns into an outdoor cinema for a fortnight in early August) is particularly popular, so book ahead. Behind the house, there's a sunny terrace and cafe overlooking the embankment.

elegant streets in London but, restrained by city planners, he couldn't realise his dream to the full. He may be disappointed, but suitably astonished, by Piccadilly Circus today: a traffic maelstrom, deluged by visitors and flanked by flashing advertisement panels. (⊖Piccadilly Circus)

Covent Garden Piazza

SQUARE

8 ◉ MAP P70, G4

London's fruit-and-vegetable wholesale market until 1974 is now mostly the preserve of visitors, who flock here to shop among the quaint old arcades, eat and drink in any of the myriad cafes and restaurants, browse through eclectic market stalls, toss coins at street performers pretending to be statues and traipse through the fun London Transport Museum (p73). On the square's western

side is handsome **St Paul's Church** (☑020-7836 5221; www.actorschurch.org; Bedford St, WC2; ⏱8.30am-5.30pm Mon-Fri, 9am-1pm Sun, hours vary Sat; ⊖Covent Garden), built in 1633. (☑020-7836 5221; ⊖Covent Garden)

All Saints

CHURCH

9 ◉ MAP P70, A1

In 1859 architect William Butterfield completed one of the country's most supreme examples of Victorian Gothic Revival architecture, enclosing the 65ft-long nave with extraordinary tiling and sumptuous stained glass. (☑020-7636 1788; www.allsaintsmargaretstreet.org.uk; 7 Margaret St, W1; ⏱7am-7pm; ⊖Oxford Circus)

St Martin-in-the-Fields

CHURCH

10 ◉ MAP P70, E5

This parish church to the royal family is a delightful fusion of neoclassical and baroque styles. It was designed by James Gibbs, completed in 1726 and served as a model for many wooden churches in New England. The church is well known for its excellent classical music concerts, many by candlelight (£9 to £30), and its links to the Chinese community (with services in English, Mandarin and Cantonese). (☑020-7766 1100; www.stmartin-in-the-fields.org; Trafalgar Sq, WC2; ⏱8.30am-1pm & 2-6pm Mon, Tue, Thu & Fri, 8.30am-1pm & 2-5pm Wed, 9.30am-6pm Sat, 3.30-5pm Sun; ⊖Charing Cross)

Chinatown

AREA

11 MAP P70, D4

Immediately north of Leicester Sq – but a world away in atmosphere – are Lisle and Gerrard Sts, focal points for London's growing Chinese community. Although not as big as Chinatowns in many other world-class cities – it's just two streets really – this is a lively quarter with Oriental gates, street signs in Chinese characters, red lanterns, restaurants and noodle shops, great Asian supermarkets and gift shops. The quality of food varies enormously, but there's a good choice of places for dim sum and other cuisines from across China and other parts of Asia. (www.chinatownlondon.org; Leicester Sq)

London Film Museum

MUSEUM

12 MAP P70, G4

This museum's star – in fact, only – attraction is its signature Bond in Motion exhibition. Get shaken and stirred at the largest official collection of 007 vehicles, including Bond's submersible Lotus Esprit (The Spy Who Loved Me), the iconic Aston Martin DB5, Goldfinger's Rolls Royce Phantom III, Timothy Dalton's Aston Martin V8 (The Living Daylights) and several of Daniel Craig's cars from Spectre. The audio tour costs £5. (020-7836 4913; www.londonfilm-museum.com; 45 Wellington St, WC2; adult/child £14.50/9.50; 10am-6pm Sun-Fri, to 7pm Sat; Covent Garden)

National Gallery & Covent Garden Sights

Covent Garden Market

PETR KOVALENKOV/SHUTTERSTOCK ©

Eating

Kanada-Ya
NOODLES £

13 ⊗ MAP P70, E2

With no reservations taken, queues can get impressive outside this tiny and enormously popular canteen, where ramen cooked in *tonkotsu* (pork bone broth) draws in diners for its three types of noodles delivered in steaming bowls, steeped in a delectable broth and highly authentic flavours. The restaurant also serves up *onigiri* (dried seaweed-wrapped rice balls; £2). (✆ 020-7240 0232; www.kanada-ya.com; 64 St Giles High St, WC2; mains £10.50-14; ⊙ noon-3pm & 5-10.30pm Mon-Sat, noon-8.30pm Sun; ⊖ Tottenham Court Rd)

Delaunay
BRASSERIE ££

14 ⊗ MAP P70, H3

This smart brasserie southeast of Covent Garden is a kind of Franco-German hybrid, where schnitzels and wieners sit happily beside croque-monsieurs and *choucroute alsacienne* (Alsace-style sauerkraut). Even more relaxed is the adjacent **Counter at the Delaunay**. (✆ 020-7499 8558; www.thedelaunay.com; 55 Aldwych, WC2; mains £7.50-35; ⊙ 7am-midnight Mon-Fri, 8am-midnight Sat, 9am-11pm Sun; ⊖; ⊖ Temple, Covent Garden)

Palomar
ISRAELI ££

15 ⊗ MAP P70, C4

The buzzing vibe at this good-looking celebration of modern-day Jerusalem cuisine (in all its permutations) is infectious, but the noise in the back dining room might drive you mad. Choose instead the counter seats at the front. The 'Yiddish-style' chopped chicken-liver pâté, the Jerusalem-style polenta and the 'octo-hummus' are all fantastic, but portions are smallish, so it's best to share several dishes. (✆ 020-7439 8777; http://thepalomar.co.uk; 34 Rupert St, W1; mains £9-17; ⊙ noon-2.30pm & 5.30-11pm Mon-Sat, 12.30-3.30pm & 6-9pm Sun; ⊖; ⊖ Piccadilly Circus)

Barrafina
SPANISH ££

16 ⊗ MAP P70, F5

With no reservations, you may need to get in line for an hour or so at this restaurant that does a brisk trade in some of the best tapas in town. Divine mouthfuls are served on each plate, from the stuffed courgette flower (£7.80) to the suckling pig's ears (£6.80) and crab on toast (£8), so would-be diners prepare to wait. (✆ 020-7440 1456; www.barrafina.co.uk; 10 Adelaide St, WC2; tapas £6.50-15.80; ⊙ noon-3pm & 5-11pm Mon-Sat, 1-3.30pm & 5.30-10pm Sun; ⊖ Embankment, Leicester Sq)

5th View
INTERNATIONAL ££

The views of Westminster from the top floor of Waterstones on Piccadilly are just the start. Add a relaxed, sophisticated dining room (see 39 ⊙ Map p70, B5) and some lovely food, and it's a gem. We love the Greek mezze and antipasti platters (£15.50) to share and the prix fixe lunch (two/

three courses £16.95/19.95, with glass of vino). (☏020-7851 2433; www.5thview.co.uk; 5th fl, Waterstone's Piccadilly, 203-206 Piccadilly, W1; mains from £8.50; 🕙9am-9.30pm Mon-Sat, noon-5pm Sun; ⊖Piccadilly Circus)

Brasserie Zédel
FRENCH ££

17 🍴 MAP P70, B5

This brasserie in the renovated art deco ballroom of a former hotel is the Frenchest eatery west of Calais. Favourites include *choucroute alsacienne* (sauerkraut with sausages and charcuterie; £15.50) or a straight-up *steak haché* (chopped steak) with pepper sauce and *frites* (£9.75). Set menus (£9.95/13.25 for two/three courses) and plats du jour (£15.75) offer excellent value in a terrific setting. (☏020-7734 4888; www. brasseriezedel.com; 20 Sherwood St, W1; mains £9.75-25.75; 🕙11.30am-midnight Mon-Sat, to 11pm Sun; 🛜; ⊖Piccadilly Circus)

Koya Bar
JAPANESE £

18 🍴 MAP P70, D3

Arrive early if you don't want to queue at this informal but excellent Japanese eatery with counter seating. Londoners come here for their fill of authentic udon noodles (served hot or cold, in soup or with a cold sauce), efficient service and very reasonable prices. The saba udon noodles with chunks of smoked mackerel and watercress is excellent. (www.koyabar.co.uk; 50 Frith St, W1; mains £7-15; 🕙8.30am-10.30pm Mon-Wed, to 11pm Thu & Fri, 9.30am-11pm Sat, to 10.30pm Sun; ⊖Tottenham Court Rd, Leicester Sq)

National Gallery & Covent Garden Eating

Brasserie Zédel

ICONIC CORNWALL/ALAMY STOCK PHOTO ©

West End on the Cheap

London, the West End especially, can be an expensive destination, but there are plenty of tricks to make your pennies last. Many of the top museums are free, so give them priority over the more commercial attractions. The West End is also compact, so walk, take the bus (cheaper than the tube) or hop on a **Santander Cycle** (📞 0343 222 6666; www.tfl.gov.uk/modes/cycling/santander-cycles). Finally, go out early – most bars in the West End offer happy hour until 8pm or 9pm.

Portrait
MODERN EUROPEAN £££

This stunningly located restaurant (see 1 ◉ Map p70, E5) above the excellent National Portrait Gallery (p72) comes with dramatic views over Trafalgar Sq and Westminster. It's a fine choice for tantalising food and the chance to relax after a morning or afternoon of picture-gazing at the gallery. The breakfast/brunch (10am to 11am) and afternoon tea (3.30pm to 4.30pm) come highly recommended. Booking is advisable. (📞 020-7312 2490; www.npg.org. uk/visit/shop-eat-drink.php; 3rd fl, National Portrait Gallery, St Martin's Pl, WC2; mains £19.50-28, 2-/3-course menu £28/31.50; ⏰ 10-11am, 11.45am-3pm & 3.30-4.30pm daily, 6.30-8.30pm Thu, Fri & Sat; 🛜; 🚇 Charing Cross)

Claridge's Foyer & Reading Room
BRITISH £££

19 🍴 MAP P70, A3

Extend that pinkie finger to partake in afternoon tea within the classic art deco foyer and Reading Room of this landmark hotel, where the gentle clink of fine porcelain and champagne glasses could be a defining memory of your trip to London. The setting is gorgeous and dress is elegant, smart casual (ripped jeans and baseball caps won't get served). (📞 020-7107 8886; www.claridges. co.uk; 49-53 Brook St, W1; afternoon tea £60, with champagne £70; ⏰ afternoon tea 2.45-5.30pm; 🛜; 🚇 Bond St)

Nordic Bakery
SCANDINAVIAN £

20 🍴 MAP P70, B4

This is the perfect place to escape the chaos that is Soho and relax in the dark-wood-panelled space on the southern side of a delightful 'undiscovered' square. Lunch on Scandinavian smoked-fish or meatball sandwiches (£4.50) or goat's cheese and beetroot salad, or have an afternoon break with tea/coffee and rustic oatmeal cookies. Get inspired by co-owner Miisa Mink's *Nordic Bakery Cookbook*. (📞 020-3230 1077; www.nordicbakery.com; 14a Golden Sq, W1; snacks £4-6; ⏰ 7.30am-8pm Mon-Fri, 8.30am-7pm Sat, 9am-7pm Sun; 🛜; 🚇 Piccadilly Circus)

Mildreds

VEGETARIAN £

21 🍴 MAP P70, B3

Central London's most inventive vegetarian restaurant, Mildreds is crammed at lunchtime so don't be shy about sharing a table in the sky-lit dining room. Expect the likes of Sri Lankan sweet-potato and cashew-nut curry, ricotta and truffle tortellini, Middle Eastern mezze, wonderfully exotic (and filling) salads and delicious stir-fries. There are also vegan and gluten-free options. (📞 020-7484 1634; www.mildreds.co.uk; 45 Lexington St, W1; mains £7-12; ⏱ noon-11pm Mon-Sat; 🛜 🍽; 🚇 Oxford Circus, Piccadilly Circus)

Dishoom

INDIAN £

22 🍴 MAP P70, E4

This branch of a highly successful mini-chain takes the fast-disappearing Iranian-style cafe of Bombay and gives it new life. Distressed with a modern twist (all ceiling fans, stained mirrors and sepia photos), you'll find yummy favourites like *sheekh kabab* and spicy chicken ruby, okra fries and snack foods, such as *bhel* (Bombay mix and puffed rice with pomegranate, onion, lime and mint).

Booking rules are complicated: groups under six only till 5.45pm and over six after that. No same-day bookings accepted. (📞 020-7420 9320; www.dishoom.com; 12 Upper St Martin's Lane, WC2; mains £5.50-11.20; ⏱ 8am-11pm Mon-Thu,

to midnight Fri, 9am-midnight Sat, to 11pm Sun; 🛜; 🚇 Covent Garden)

J Sheekey

SEAFOOD £££

23 🍴 MAP P70, E4

A jewel of the local dining scene, this incredibly smart restaurant, whose pedigree stretches back to the closing years of the 19th century, has four elegant, discreet and spacious wood-panelled rooms in which to savour the riches of the sea, cooked simply and exquisitely. The three-course weekend lunch is £28.75.

The **Atlantic Bar** (noon to midnight Monday to Saturday, from 5pm Sunday), popular with pre- and post-theatre goers for its oysters and shellfish, is another highlight. (📞 020-7240 2565; www.j-sheekey.co.uk; 28-32 St Martin's Ct, WC2; mains £17.50-44; ⏱ noon-3pm & 5.30pm-midnight Mon-Sat, noon-3pm & 5.30-10.30pm Sun; 🛜; 🚇 Leicester Sq)

Drinking

American Bar

BAR

24 🍺 MAP P70, A2

Sip a bourbon or a cocktail in the classic 1930s art deco ambience of this stylish bar at the hallmark Beaumont hotel. It's central, period and like a gentleman's club, but far from stuffy. Only a few years old, the American Bar feels like it's been pouring drinks since the days of the flapper and jazz age. (www.thebeaumont.com/dining/american-bar; The Beaumont,

Lamb & Flag

Brown Hart Gardens, W1; ⏱11.30am-
midnight Mon-Sat, to 11pm Sun; 📶;
Ⓔ Bond St)

American Bar COCKTAIL BAR

25 Ⓜ MAP P70, H5

Home of the Hanky Panky, White
Lady and other classic infusions
created on-site, the seriously
dishy and elegant American Bar
is an icon of London, with soft
blue and rust art deco lines and
live piano music. Cocktails start
at £17.50 and peak at a stupefying £5000 (the Original Sazerac,
containing Sazerac de Forge
cognac from 1857). (📞020-7836
4343; www.fairmont.com/savoy-lon-
don/dining/americanbar; Savoy, The
Strand, WC2; ⏱11.30am-midnight
Mon-Sat, noon-midnight Sun;
Ⓔ Covent Garden)

Lamb & Flag PUB

26 Ⓜ MAP P70, F4

Everybody's favourite pub in
central London, pint-sized Lamb
& Flag is full of charm and history,
and is on the site of a pub that
dates from at least 1772. Rain or
shine, you'll have to elbow your
way to the bar through the merry
crowd drinking outside. Inside are
brass fittings and creaky wooden
floors. (📞020-7497 9504; www.
lambandflagcoventgarden.co.uk; 33
Rose St, WC2; ⏱11am-11pm Mon-Sat,
noon-10.30pm Sun; Ⓔ Covent Garden)

Gordon's Wine Bar BAR

27 Ⓜ MAP P70, G6

Cavernous, candlelit and atmospheric, Gordon's (founded in 1890)
is a victim of its own success – it's

relentlessly busy and unless you arrive before the office crowd does (around 6pm), forget about landing a table. The French and New World wines are heady and reasonably priced; buy by the glass, the beaker (12cL), the schooner (15cL) or the bottle. (☏020-7930 1408; https://gordonswinebar.com; 47 Villiers St, WC2; ⏱11am-11pm Mon-Sat, noon-10pm Sun; ⊖Embankment, Charing Cross)

Heaven

CLUB, GAY

28 ▣ MAP P70, F6

This perennially popular mixed/gay club under the arches beneath Charing Cross Station is host to excellent live gigs and club nights. Monday's Popcorn (mixed dance party, with an all-welcome door policy) offers one of the best weeknight's clubbing in the capital. The celebrated G-A-Y takes place here on Thursday (G-A-Y Porn Idol), Friday (G-A-Y Camp Attack) and Saturday (plain ol' G-A-Y). (http://heaven-live.co.uk; Villiers St, WC2; ⏱11pm-5am Mon, to 4am Thu & Fri, 10.30pm-5am Sat; ⊖Embankment, Charing Cross)

Entertainment

Pizza Express Jazz Club

JAZZ

29 ⭐ MAP P70, C2

Pizza Express has been one of the best jazz venues in London since opening in 1969. It may be a strange arrangement, in a basement beneath a branch of the chain restaurant, but it's highly popular. Lots of big names perform here and promising artists such as Norah Jones, Gregory Porter and the late Amy Winehouse played here in their early days. (☏020-7439 4962; www.pizzaexpresslive.com/venues/soho-jazz-club; 10 Dean St, W1; tickets £15-40; ⊖Tottenham Court Rd)

Wigmore Hall

CLASSICAL MUSIC

30 ⭐ MAP P70, A1

This is one of the best and most active (more than 400 concerts

---

West End Budget Flicks

Leicester Sq cinema-ticket prices are very high, so wait until the first-runs have moved to the **Prince Charles Cinema** (Map p70, D4; www.princecharlescinema.com; 7 Leicester Pl, WC2; tickets £5-16; ⊖Leicester Sq), central London's cheapest cinema, where non-members pay only £9 to £11.50 for new releases. Also on the cards are mini-festivals, Q&As with film directors, classics, sleepover movie marathons and exuberant sing-along screenings of films like *Frozen*, *The Sound of Music* and *Rocky Horror Picture Show* (£16).

a year) classical-music venues in town, not only because of its fantastic acoustics, beautiful art nouveau hall and great variety of concerts and recitals, but also because of the sheer standard of the performances. Built in 1901, it has remained one of the world's top places for chamber music. (www.wigmore-hall.org.uk; 36 Wigmore St, W1; ⊖ Bond St)

Royal Opera House   OPERA

31 ⭐ MAP P70, G3

Classic opera in London has a fantastic setting on Covent Garden Piazza and coming here for a night is a sumptuous – if pricey – affair. Although the program has been fluffed up by modern influences, the main attractions are still the opera and classical ballet – all are wonderful productions and feature world-class performers. (☎ 020-7304 4000; www.roh.org.uk; Bow St, WC2; tickets £4-270; ⊖ Covent Garden)

Ronnie Scott's   JAZZ

32 ⭐ MAP P70, D3

Ronnie Scott's jazz club opened in 1965 and became widely known as Britain's best. Support acts are at 7pm, with main gigs at 8.15pm (8pm Sunday) and a second house at 11.15pm Friday and Saturday (check ahead). The more informal Late, Late Show runs from 1am to 3am. Expect to pay from £25; the Late, Late Show and Sunday lunch shows are just £10. (☎ 020-7439 0747; www.ronniescotts.co.uk; 47 Frith St, W1; ⊙ 7pm-3am Mon-Sat, 1-4pm & 8pm-midnight Sun; ⊖ Leicester Sq, Tottenham Court Rd)

Wigmore Hall (p81)

Comedy Store COMEDY

33 ⭐ MAP P70, C5

This is one of the first (and still one of the best) comedy clubs in London. Wednesday and Sunday night's Comedy Store Players is the most famous improvisation outfit in town, with the wonderful Josie Lawrence, now a veteran of two decades. On Thursdays, Fridays and Saturdays, Best in Stand Up features the best on London's comedy circuit.

Doors at 6.30pm; show kicks off at 8pm. Tickets cost from £8 for King Gong (an open-mic night every Monday of the month) to £22.50 (best seats for Best in Stand Up show on Saturdays). (📞0844 871 7699; www.thecomedy store.co.uk; 1a Oxendon St, SW1; tickets £8-22.50; ⊖Piccadilly Circus)

Borderline LIVE MUSIC

34 ⭐ MAP P70, D2

Through the hard-to-find entrance off Orange Yard and down into the basement you'll find a packed, 275-capacity venue that really punches above its weight. Read the gig list: Ed Sheeran, REM, Blur, Counting Crows, PJ Harvey, Lenny Kravitz and Pearl Jam, plus many anonymous indie outfits, have all played here. The crowd's equally diverse but can contain music journos and record-company talent spotters.

Gigs (£7 to £12) are usually at 7pm Tuesday to Saturday, with an additional one at 11pm on Friday and Saturday. (📞020-7734 5547; http://

borderline.london; Orange Yard, off Manette St, W1; ⊖Tottenham Court Rd)

Shopping

Fortnum & Mason DEPARTMENT STORE

35 🔒 MAP P70, A6

With its classic eau-de-Nil (pale green) colour scheme, 'the Queen's grocery store' established in 1707 refuses to yield to modern times. Its staff – men and women – still wear old-fashioned tailcoats and its glamorous food hall is supplied with hampers, marmalades, speciality teas, superior fruitcakes and so forth. Fortnum & Mason remains the quintessential London shopping experience. (📞020-7734 8040; www.fortnumandmason.com; 181 Piccadilly, W1; ⊙10am-8pm Mon-Sat, 11.30am-6pm Sun; ⊖Piccadilly Circus)

Hatchards BOOKS

36 🔒 MAP P70, B6

London's oldest bookshop dates back to 1797. Holding three royal warrants, it's a stupendous bookshop now in the Waterstones (a British book retailer) stable, with a solid supply of signed editions and bursting at its smart seams with very browsable stock. There's a strong selection of 1st editions on the ground floor and regularly scheduled literary events. (📞020-7439 9921; www.hatchards.co.uk; 187 Piccadilly, W1; ⊙9.30am-8pm Mon-Sat, noon-6.30pm Sun; ⊖Green Park, Piccadilly Circus)

Liberty
DEPARTMENT STORE

37 🏠 MAP P70, A3

An irresistible blend of contemporary styles in an old-fashioned mock-Tudor atmosphere (1875), Liberty has a huge cosmetics department and an accessories floor, along with a breathtaking lingerie section, all at sky-high prices. A classic London gift or souvenir is a Liberty fabric print, especially in the form of a scarf. (📞020-7734 1234; www.liberty.co.uk; Great Marlborough St, W1; ⏰10am-8pm Mon-Sat, noon-6pm Sun; 🚇Oxford Circus)

Penhaligon's
PERFUME

38 🏠 MAP P70, A6

Located in the historic Burlington Arcade (p57), Penhaligon's is a classic British perfumery. Attendants enquire about your favourite smells, take you on an exploratory tour of the shop's signature range, and help you discover new scents in their traditional perfumes, home fragrances and bath and body products. Everything is produced in England. (📞020-7629 1416; www.penhaligons.com; 16-17 Burlington Arcade, W1; ⏰9am-6.30pm Mon-Fri, 9.30am-6.30pm Sat, noon-6pm Sun; 🚇Piccadilly Circus, Green Park)

Waterstones Piccadilly
BOOKS

39 🏠 MAP P70, B5

The chain's megastore is the largest bookshop in Europe, with helpful, knowledgeable staff and regular author readings, signings and discussions. The store spreads across eight floors, with a fabulous rooftop bar-restaurant,

Hamleys

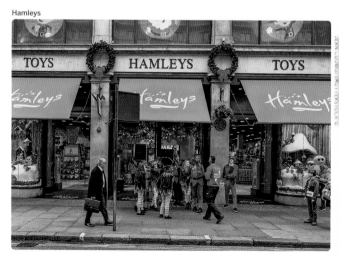

Regent Street

The handsome border dividing trainer-clad clubbers of Soho from the Gucci-heeled hedge-fund managers of Mayfair, Regent St was designed by John Nash as a ceremonial route linking Carlton House, the Prince Regent's long-demolished town residence, with the 'wilds' of Regent's Park. Nash had to downsize his plan and build the thoroughfare on a curve, but Regent St is today a well-subscribed shopping street lined with some lovely listed buildings.

Its anchor tenant is undoubtedly **Hamleys**, London's premier toy and game store. Regent St is also famous for its **Christmas light displays**, which get glowing with great pomp earlier and earlier (or so it seems) each year (usually around mid-November). The street is closed to traffic each Sunday in July for the so-called Summer Streets celebration.

5th View (p76), and Cafe W in the basement. (☎020-7851 2433; www.waterstones.com; 203-206 Piccadilly, W1; ⏱9am-9.30pm Mon-Sat, noon-5pm Sun; ⊖Piccadilly Circus)

Hamleys   TOYS

40 🔒 MAP P70, A4

Claiming to be the world's oldest (and some say, largest) toy store, Hamleys moved to its address on Regent St in 1881. From the basement's Star Wars Collection and ground floor where staff blow bubbles and glide foam boomerangs through the air with practised nonchalance to Lego World and a cafe on the 5th floor, it's a rich layer cake of playthings. (☎0371 704 1977; www.hamleys.com; 188-196 Regent St, W1; ⏱10am-9pm Mon-Fri, 9.30am-9pm Sat, noon-6pm Sun; ⊖Oxford Circus)

Explore ⊗

British Museum & Bloomsbury

Bookish Bloomsbury puts a leisurely and genteel spin on central London. Home to the British Museum, the British Library, universities, publishing houses, literary pubs and gorgeous Georgian squares, Bloomsbury is deeply but accessibly cultured. You could spend all day in the British Museum, but there's a tantalising choice of options outside, with excellent pubs and restaurants nearby.

The British Museum (p88) is one of Britain's top sights, so arrive early to do it justice. You will need at least the entire morning here to make any headway. Have lunch locally before ambling down to King's Cross. Bibliophiles and library lovers will find the British Library (p96) a true eye-opener. Bloomsbury has an alluring selection of international restaurants for dinner, such as Hakkasan (p100). Embark on a pub crawl through the neighbourhood's historic and literary watering holes, or check out the program at The Place (p104) for cutting-edge dance shows.

Getting There & Around

◉ Get off at Tottenham Court Rd (Northern and Central Lines), Goodge St (Northern Line), Russell Sq (Piccadilly Line) or Euston Sq (Circle, Hammersmith & City and Metropolitan Lines).

🚌 For the British Museum and Russell Sq, take bus 98 along Oxford St; bus 91 runs from Whitehall/Trafalgar Sq to the British Library.

Bloomsbury Map on p94

British Library (p96) GRAPHICAL_BANK/SHUTTERSTOCK ©

Top Sight 📷
British Museum

Britain's most visited attraction for a decade, the British Museum draws in 6.5 million visitors each year. It's an exhaustive and exhilarating stampede through world cultures over 7000 years, with 90 galleries of seven million exhibits devoted to ancient civilisations, from Egypt to western Asia, the Middle East, Rome and Greece, India, Africa, prehistoric and Roman Britain, and medieval antiquities.

◉ MAP P94, C7

www.britishmuseum.org

Great Russell St & Montague Pl, WC1

admission free

🕑 10am-5.30pm Sat-Thu, to 8.30pm Fri

🚇 Russell Sq, Tottenham Court Rd

History of the Museum

The museum was founded in 1753 when royal physician Hans Sloane sold his 'cabinet of curiosities' for the then-princely sum of £20,000, raised by national lottery. The collection opened to the public for free in 1759, and the museum has since kept expanding its collection through judicious acquisitions, bequests and the controversial imperial plundering.

The Great Court

The first thing you'll see on entry is the Great Court covered with a spectacular glass-and-steel roof designed by Norman Foster in 2000. It is the largest covered public square in Europe. In its centre is the celebrated **Reading Room**, once part of the British Library, which has been frequented by the big brains of history, from Mahatma Gandhi to Karl Marx. It is now used for temporary exhibits.

Enlightenment Galleries

Formerly known as the King's Library, this stunning neoclassical space (room 1) just off the Great Court was built between 1823 and 1827 and was the first part of the new museum building as it is seen today. Through a fascinating collection of artefacts, the collection traces how such disciplines as biology, archaeology, linguistics and geography emerged during the Enlightenment of the 18th century.

Ancient Egypt

The star of the show is the Ancient Egypt collection upstairs. It comprises sculptures, fine jewellery, papyrus texts, coffins and mummies, including the beautiful and intriguing Mummy of Katebet (room 63). The most prized item in the museum is the **Rosetta Stone** (room 4), the key to deciphering Egyptian hieroglyphics. In the same gallery is the enormous bust of the pharaoh **Ramesses II** (room 4).

★ **Top Tips**

○ The British Museum has two entrances: one on Great Russell St and the other on Montague Pl (usually less busy).

○ Do not attempt to see all sections of the museum; there are more than 5km of corridors. Instead, choose one or two periods or civilisations (eg Ancient Egypt, Roman Britain, Japan and Korea).

✕ **Take a Break**

The British Museum is vast so you'll need to recharge. **Abeno** (www.abeno.co.uk; 47 Museum St, WC1; mains £9.75-26.80; ⊙ noon-10pm) is nearby for scrumptious savoury pancakes and other dishes from Japan.

For something more traditional, enjoy a cream tea at **Tea & Tattle** (www.apandtea.co.uk; 41 Great Russell St, WC1; afternoon tea for one/two £17/33.50; ⊙ 9am-6.30pm Mon-Fri, noon-4pm Sat; ☎), which is just across the road.

Assyrian Treasures

Assyrian treasures from ancient Mesopotamia include the **Winged Bulls** from Khorsabad (room 10). Behind it are the exquisite **Lion Hunt Reliefs** from Ninevah (room 10) dating from the 7th century BC, which influenced Greek sculpture. Such antiquities are all the more significant after the so-called Islamic State's bulldozing of Nimrud in 2015.

Parthenon Sculptures

A major highlight of the museum is the Parthenon sculptures (room 18). The 80m-long marble frieze is thought to be of the Great Panathenaea, a version of a festival in honour of Athena held every four years.

Mildenhall Treasure & Lindow Man

Upstairs are finds from Britain and the rest of Europe (rooms 40 to 51). Many go back to Roman times, when the empire spread across much of the continent, including the Mildenhall Treasure (room 49), a collection of almost three-dozen pieces of 4th-century-AD Roman silverware unearthed in Suffolk with both pagan and early-Christian motifs. Lindow Man (room 50) is the well-preserved remains of a 1st-century man discovered in a bog near Manchester in northern England in 1984.

Sutton Hoo Ship Burial

The medieval artefacts from the Sutton Hoo Ship Burial (room 41), an elaborate Anglo-Saxon burial site from Suffolk dating back to the 7th century, are another unmissable highlight of the museum.

Lewis Chessmen

Perennial favourites are the lovely Lewis Chessmen (room 40), some 78 12th-century game pieces carved from walrus tusk and whale teeth that were found on a remote Scottish island in the early 19th century.

Museum Extension

The British Museum's long-awaited extension, the £135 million World Conservation & Exhibitions Centre, opened in 2014, in the same year as the Sainsbury Exhibitions Gallery, which hosts high-profile exhibitions.

British Museum

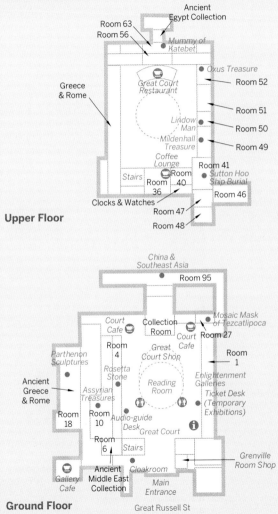

Upper Floor

- Room 63
- Room 56
- Ancient Egypt Collection
- Mummy of Katebet
- Oxus Treasure
- Room 52
- Greece & Rome
- Great Court Restaurant
- Room 51
- Room 50
- Lindow Man
- Room 49
- Mildenhall Treasure
- Coffee Lounge
- Room 41
- Sutton Hoo Ship Burial
- Stairs
- Room 40
- Room 36
- Room 46
- Clocks & Watches
- Room 47
- Room 48

Ground Floor

- China & Southeast Asia
- Room 95
- Court Cafe
- Collection Room
- Mosaic Mask of Tezcatlipoca
- Room 4
- Court Cafe
- Room 27
- Parthenon Sculptures
- Great Court Shop
- Room 1
- Rosetta Stone
- Reading Room
- Enlightenment Galleries
- Ancient Greece & Rome
- Assyrian Treasures
- Ticket Desk (Temporary Exhibitions)
- Room 18
- Room 10
- Audio-guide Desk
- Great Court
- Room 6
- Stairs
- Gallery Cafe
- Ancient Middle East Collection
- Cloakroom
- Grenville Room Shop
- Main Entrance
- Great Russell St

Walking Tour 🥾

A Literary Walk Around Bloomsbury

Bloomsbury is indelibly associated with the literary circles that made this part of London their home. Charles Dickens, JM Barrie, WB Yeats, Virginia Woolf, TS Eliot, Sylvia Plath and other bold-faced names of English literature all have their names associated with properties delightfully dotted around Bloomsbury and its attractive squares.

Walk Facts

Start Bedford Sq;
🚇 Goodge St

End Museum Tavern;
🚇 Holborn or Tottenham

Length 1.8km; two to three hours

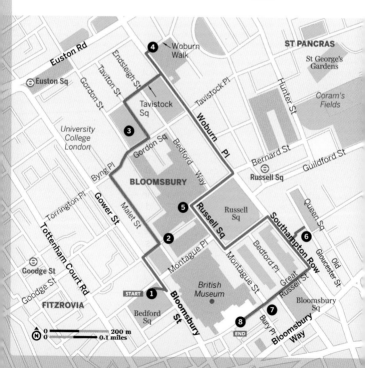

❶ Bedford Square

An eye-catching symbiosis of Bloomsbury's creative heritage and architectural charms, Bedford Sq is London's best-preserved Georgian square. The main office of publishing house Bloomsbury Publishing is at No 50. Sir Anthony Hope Hawkins, author of *The Prisoner of Zenda*, lived at No 41 while the Pre-Raphaelite Brotherhood was founded around the corner at 7 Gower St in 1848.

❷ Senate House

Along student-thronged Malet St, the splendid but intimidating art deco Senate House served as the Ministry of Information in WWII, providing the inspiration for George Orwell's Ministry of Truth in his dystopian 1948 novel, *Nineteen Eighty-Four*. Orwell's wife, Eileen, worked in the censorship department between 1939 and 1942.

❸ Gordon Square

Once a private square, Gordon Sq is open to the public and a lovely place for a rest. It is filled with blue plaques attesting to the presence of literary greatness.

❹ WB Yeats & Woburn Walk

Irish poet and playwright WB Yeats lived at 5 Woburn Walk, a genteel lane just south of the church of St Pancras. A leading figure of the Celtic Revival, which promoted the native heritage of Ireland, and author of *The Tower*, WB Yeats was born in Dublin, but spent many years in London.

❺ Faber & Faber

The former offices of Faber & Faber are at the northwest corner of Russell Sq, marked with a blue plaque about TS Eliot, the American poet and playwright and first editor at Faber. The gardens and towering fountain at the centre of Russell Sq are excellent for recuperation.

❻ St George the Martyr

The 18th-century church of St George the Martyr, across from the historic **Queen's Larder** (p102) pub at the south end of Queen Sq, was where Ted Hughes and Sylvia Plath were married on 16 June in 1956 (aka Bloomsday). The couple chose this date to tie the knot in honour of James Joyce.

❼ Literary Shopping

It wouldn't be Bloomsbury without a good bookshop and the **London Review Bookshop** (p105) is one of London's finest. Affiliated with literary magazine *London Review of Books*, it features an eclectic selection of books and DVDs. Bookworms spend hours browsing the shelves or absorbed in new purchases in the shop's cafe.

❽ Drinks at Museum Tavern

Finish of your walk with a well-earned pint at the Museum Tavern (p102), just as Karl Marx used to do.

British Museum & Bloomsbury

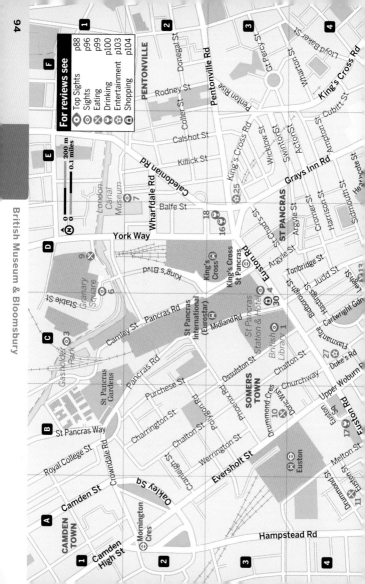

For reviews see

◎	Top Sights	p88
◉	Sights	p96
⊗	Eating	p99
⊗	Drinking	p100
⊗	Entertainment	p103
⊕	Shopping	p104

0 ——— 200 m
0 ——— 0.1 miles

CAMDEN TOWN

PENTONVILLE

SOMERS TOWN

ST PANCRAS

King's Cross

Euston

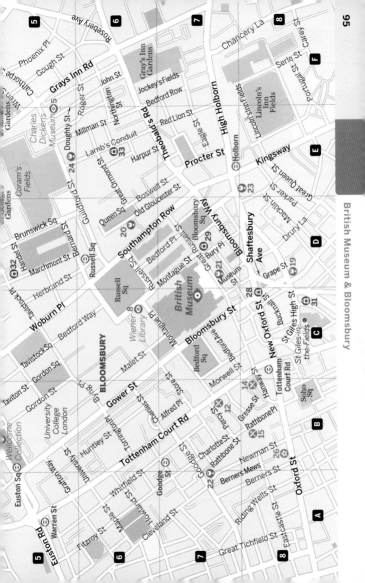

Sights

British Library
LIBRARY

1 MAP P94, C3

Consisting of low-slung red-brick terraces and fronted by a large plaza featuring an oversized statue of Sir Isaac Newton, Colin St John Wilson's British Library building is a love-it-or-hate-it affair. Completed in 1997, it's home to some of the greatest treasures of the written word, including the *Codex Sinaiticus* (the first complete text of the New Testament), Leonardo da Vinci's notebooks and a copy of the Magna Carta (1215). (www.bl.uk; 96 Euston Rd, NW1; admission free; ⏰galleries 9.30am-6pm Mon & Wed-Fri, to 8pm Tue, to 5pm Sat, 11am-5pm Sun; 🚇King's Cross St Pancras)

Wellcome Collection
MUSEUM

2 MAP P94, B5

Focusing on the interface of art, science and medicine, this clever and resourceful museum is fascinating. The heart of the museum is Sir Henry Wellcome's collec-

tion of medical curiosities (saws for amputation, forceps through the ages, sex aids and amulets etc), which illustrate the universal fascination with health and the body across civilisations. In the **Medicine Now** gallery, interactive displays and provocative artworks are designed to make you ponder about humanity and the human body. (www.wellcomecollection.org; 183 Euston Rd, NW1; admission free; ⏰10am-6pm Tue, Wed & Fri-Sun, to 10pm Thu; 🚇Euston Sq, Euston)

Gasholder Park
PARK

3 MAP P94, C1

Part of the impressive redevelopment of the King's Cross area, this urban green space right by Regent's Canal is a masterpiece of regeneration. The cast iron structure used to be the frame of Gasholder No 8, the largest gas storage cylinder in the area (which was originally located across the canal). Carefully renovated, and with the addition of a central lawn, beautiful benches and a mirrored canopy, it has metamorphosed into a gorgeous pocket park. (🚇King's Cross St Pancras)

St Pancras Station & Hotel
HISTORIC BUILDING

4 MAP P94, D3

Looking at the jaw-dropping Gothic splendour of St Pancras, it's hard to believe that the 1873 Midland Grand Hotel languished empty for years and even faced demolition in the 1960s. Now home to a five-star hotel, 67 luxury apartments and

Surf & Rest

The British Library has free wi-fi throughout the building, making it a favoured hang-out for students, but visitors can also take advantage of the service while enjoying a break in one of the library's three excellent cafes and restaurants.

Granary Square

the Eurostar terminal, the entire complex has been returned to its former glory. Tours (£20; 10.30am, noon, 2pm and 3.30pm weekends) take you on a fascinating journey through the building's history, from its inception as the southern terminus for the Midlands Railway line. (☎020-8241 6921; www. stpancraslondon.com; Euston Rd, NW1; ☻King's Cross St Pancras)

Charles Dickens Museum

MUSEUM

5 ◉ MAP P94, E5

A £3.5 million renovation funded by the Heritage Lottery Fund has made this museum – located in a handsome four-storey house that is the beloved Victorian novelist's sole surviving residence in Lon-

don – bigger and better than ever. A period kitchen in the basement and a nursery in the attic were added, and newly acquired 49 Doughty St increased the exhibition space substantially. (☎020-7405 2127; www.dickensmuseum.com; 48 Doughty St, WC1; adult/child £9/4; ☻10am-5pm Tue-Sun; ☻Chancery Lane, Russell Sq)

Granary Square

SQUARE

6 ◉ MAP P94, D1

Positioned by a sharp bend in the Regent's Canal north of King's Cross Station, Granary Sq is at the heart of a major redevelopment of a 27-hectare expanse once full of abandoned freight warehouses. Its most striking feature is a fountain made of 1080 individually lit water jets, which pulse and dance in

St Giles-in-the-Fields: A Litany of Miseries

Built in what used to be countryside between the City of London and Westminster, **St Giles-in-the-Fields** (Map p94, C8; ☎020-7240 2532; www.stgilesonline.org; 60 St Giles High St, WC2; ☺9am-4.30pm Mon-Fri; ⊖Tottenham Court Rd) isn't much to look at but its history is a chronicle of London's most miserable inhabitants. The current structure (1733) is the third to stand on the site of an original chapel built in the 12th century to serve as a hospital for lepers.

Until 1547, when the hospital closed, prisoners on their way to be executed at the Tyburn Tree stopped at the church gate and sipped a large cup of soporific ale – their last refreshment – from St Giles's Bowl. From 1650, the prisoners were buried in the church grounds. It was also within the boundaries of St Giles that the Great Plague of 1665 took hold.

In Victorian times, it was London's worst slum, often mentioned in Dickens' novels. Today the drug users who hang out around the area make it feel like things haven't changed much.

An interesting relic in the church (northern side) is the plain white pulpit that was used for 40 years by John Wesley, the founder of Methodism.

sequence. On hot spring and summer days, it becomes a busy urban beach. (www.kingscross.co.uk; Stable St, N1; ⊖King's Cross St Pancras)

London Canal Museum

MUSEUM

7 ◉ MAP P94, E2

This little museum traces the history of the Regent's Canal and explores what life was like for families living and working on Britain's impressively long and historic canal system. The exhibits in the stables upstairs are dedicated to the history of canal transport in Britain, including recent developments such as the clean up of the Lea River for the 2012 Olympic Games. The museum is housed in a warehouse dating from 1858, where ice was once stored in two deep wells. (☎020-7713 0836; www.canalmuseum.org.uk; 12-13 New Wharf Rd, N1; adult/child £5/2.50; ☺10am-4.30pm Tue-Sun & bank holidays; ⊖King's Cross St Pancras)

Wiener Library

MUSEUM

8 ◉ MAP P94, C6

The Wiener Library was established in 1933 by a German Jew called Alfred Wiener to document the rise of anti-Semitism in his home country, from which he had fled in the face of Nazi persecution. It's the world's oldest institution dedicated to the study of the

Holocaust. Now a public library and research institute, it contains over a million items relating to one of history's darkest periods. (📞020-7636 7247; www.wienerlibrary. co.uk; 29 Russell Sq, WC1; admission free; 🕐10am-5pm Mon & Wed-Fri, to 7.30pm Tue; 🚇Russell Square)

Eating

Ruby Violet   ICE CREAM £

9 ❌ MAP P94, D1

This parlour is taking ice cream to the next level: flavours are wonderfully original (masala chai, Belgian chocolate, raspberry and sweet potato) and toppings and hot sauces are house-made. Plus, there's Pudding Club on Friday and Saturday nights, when you can sink your spoon into a mini baked Alaska or hot chocolate fondant and ice cream. (www. rubyviolet.co.uk; Midlands Goods Shed, 3 Wharf Rd, N1C; 1/2 scoops £3/5.50; 🕐10am-7pm Sun-Thu, to 10pm Fri & Sat; 🚇King's Cross St Pancras)

Roti King   MALAYSIAN £

10 ❌ MAP P94, B3

The neon sign pointing you in the direction of this pocket-sized basement restaurant doesn't look too promising. Step inside the white-tiled eatery, however, and you know you're in safe hands. It's all about roti canai, a flaky flatbread typical of Malaysia, served with fragrant bowls of curry or stuffed with tasty fillings. A genuine budget option that isn't a sandwich or a salad – hurrah. (40 Doric Way, NW1; mains £5-7; 🕐noon-3pm & 5-10.30pm Mon-Fri, noon-10.30pm Sat; 🚇Euston)

Diwana Bhel Poori House   INDIAN £

11 ❌ MAP P94, A4

One of the best Indian vegetarian restaurants in London, Diwana specialises in Bombay-style *bhel poori* (a tangy, soft and crunchy 'party mix' dish) and *dosas* (filled crispy pancakes made from rice flour). Solo diners should consider a *thali* (a complete meal consisting of lots of small dishes). The all-you-can-eat lunchtime buffet (£7) is legendary, and there are daily specials (£6.60). (📞020-7387 5556; www.diwanabph.com; 121-123 Drummond St, NW1; mains £5.10-8.95; 🕐noon-11.30pm Mon-Sat, to 10.30pm Sun; 🖈; 🚇Euston)

Sagar   VEGETARIAN £

12 ❌ MAP P94, B7

This branch of a mini-chain specialises in vegetarian dishes from the southern Indian state of Karnataka. It's cheap, filling and of a fine standard. Try the paper masala dosa, an enormous lentil pancake with spicy potato filling. Thalis – steel trays with a selection of small dishes – are £16 to £18. (📞020-7631 3319; www.sagarveg.co.uk; 17a Percy St, W1; mains £5.50-9.45; 🕐noon-3pm & 5.30-10.45pm Mon-Thu, noon-11pm Fri & Sat, noon-10pm Sun; 🖈; 🚇Tottenham Court Rd)

North Sea Fish Restaurant

FISH & CHIPS ££

13 🍴 MAP P94, D4

The North Sea sets out to cook fresh fish and potatoes – a simple ambition in which it succeeds admirably. Look forward to jumbo-sized plaice or halibut fillets, deep-fried or grilled, and a huge serving of chips. There's takeaway next door with similar hours if you can't face the rather austere dining room and faceless service. (📞020-7387 5892; www.northseafishrestaurant. co.uk; 7-8 Leigh St, WC1; mains £10-25; ⏰noon-2.30pm & 5-10pm Mon-Sat, 5-9.30pm Sun; ⊖Russell Sq)

Hakkasan Hanway Place

CANTONESE £££

14 🍴 MAP P94, B8

This basement Michelin-starred restaurant – hidden down a back alleyway – successfully combines celebrity status, stunning design, persuasive cocktails and sophisticated Cantonese-style food. The low, nightclub-style lighting makes it a good spot for a date or a night out with friends; the bar serves seriously creative cocktails. Book far in advance or come for lunch (three courses £38, also available from 5.30pm to 6.30pm). (📞020-7927 7000; www.hakkasan.com; 8 Hanway Pl, W1; mains £12-63.50; ⏰noon-3pm & 5.30-11pm Mon-Wed, noon-3pm & 5.30pm-12.30am Thu-Fri, noon-4pm & 5.30pm-12.30am Sat, noon-11.15pm Sun; 📶; ⊖Tottenham Court Rd)

Lima

PERUVIAN £££

15 🍴 MAP P94, B8

Sublimely zestful and piquant Peruvian flavours percolate at the heart of this fantastic restaurant with a large colourful mural. The stunningly presented cuisine has pulled a Michelin star, while helpful staff take pride in their work. Express lunch with a glass of wine is a snip at £19. (📞020-3002 2640; www.limalondon.com; 31 Rathbone Pl, W1; mains £22-32; ⏰noon-2.30pm Mon-Fri, 11.30am-2.30pm Sat & Sun, 5.30-10.30pm Mon-Sat, to 9.30pm Sun; 📶; ⊖Tottenham Court Rd)

Drinking

Bar Pepito

WINE BAR

16 🍺 MAP P94, D3

This tiny, intimate Andalusian bodega specialises in sherry and tapas. Novices fear not: the staff are on hand to advise. They're also experts at food pairings (top-notch ham and cheese selections). To go the whole hog, try a tasting flight of selected sherries with snacks to match. (www.camino.uk.com/location/bar-pepito; 3 Varnishers Yard, The Regent's Quarter, N1; ⏰5pm-midnight Mon-Fri, 6pm-midnight Sat; ⊖King's Cross St Pancras)

Euston Tap

BAR

17 🍺 MAP P94, B4

This specialist drinking spot inhabits a monumental stone structure on the approach to Euston Station. Craft-beer devotees can choose between 16 cask ales, 25 keg beers and 150 brews by the bottle. Grab a seat on the pavement, take the tight spiral staircase upstairs or buy a bottle to take away. (📞 020-3137 8837; www.eustontap.com; 190 Euston Rd, NW1; 🕐 noon-11pm Mon-Sat, to 10pm Sun; 🚇 Euston)

Drink, Shop & Do
BAR

18 🅑 MAP P94, D3

This kooky little outlet will not be pigeonholed. As its name suggests, it is many things to many people: a bar, a cafe, an activities centre, a disco even. But the idea is that there will always be drinking (be it tea or gin), music and things to do – anything from dancing to building Lego robots. (📞 020-7278 4335; www.

drinkshopdo.co.uk; 9 Caledonian Rd, N1; 🕐 7.30am-midnight Mon-Thu, 7.30am-2am Fri, 10.30am-2am Sat, to 6pm Sun; 📶; 🚇 King's Cross St Pancras)

Craft Beer Company
CRAFT BEER

19 🅟 MAP P94, D8

Probably the best place to go in London to enjoy craft beer, this branch of a six-strong chain boasts 15 cask pumps of UK-sourced beers as well as 30 keg lines and 200-plus bottles and cans of beers from around the world. Most pints are under £5. (📞 020-7240 0431; www.thecraft-beerco.com/covent-garden; 168 High Holborn, WC1; 🕐 noon-midnight Sun-Wed, to 1am Thu-Sat; 🚇 Tottenham Court Rd)

British Museum & Bloomsbury Drinking

Queen's Larder

London's Bewildering Postcodes 👍

Just take a look at the 20 arrondissements in Paris that spiral clockwise from the centre in such a lovely – and logical – fashion. If you've got a letter for someone in the 5th, you simply write 75005. Now take a look at London's codes on a map. How on Earth can SE23 border SE6? If there's a north (N), a west (W) and an east (E), why isn't there a south (S)? And what happened to the northeast (NE)?

When they were introduced in 1858, the postcodes were fairly clear, with all the compass points represented, along with an east and west central (EC and WC). But not long afterwards NE was merged with E and S with SE and SW, and the problems began. The real convolution came during WWI when a numbering system was introduced for inexperienced sorters (regular employees were off fighting in 'the war to end all wars'). No 1 was the centre of each zone, but other numbers related to the alphabetical order of the postal districts' names. Thus anything starting with a letter near the beginning of the alphabet, like Chingford in East London, would get a low number (E4), even though it was miles from the centre at Whitechapel (E1), while Poplar, which borders Whitechapel, got E14. It's still mind-boggling.

Queen's Larder   PUB

20 🚇 MAP P94, D6

In a lovely square southeast of Russell Sq is this cosy pub, so called because Queen Charlotte, wife of 'Mad' King George III, rented part of the pub's cellar to store special foods for her husband while he was being treated nearby for what is now believed to have been the genetic disease porphyria. There are benches outside and a dining room upstairs. (📞020-7837 5627; www.queenslarder. co.uk; 1 Queen Sq, WC1; ⊙11.30am-11pm Mon-Fri, noon-11pm Sat, noon-10.30pm Sun; 🚇Russell Sq)

Museum Tavern   PUB

21 🚇 MAP P94, D7

Karl Marx used to tarry here for a well-earned pint after a hard day inventing communism in the British Museum's Reading Room; George Orwell also boozed here, as did Sir Arthur Conan Doyle and JB Priestley. A lovely traditional pub set around a long bar, it has friendly staff and period features, and is popular with academics and students alike. (📞020-7242 8987; www. taylor-walker.co.uk/pub/museum-tavern-bloomsbury/c0747; 49 Great Russell St, WC1; ⊙11am-11.30pm Mon-Thu, to midnight Fri & Sat, noon-10.30pm Sun; 🛜; 🚇Holborn, Tottenham Court Rd)

London Cocktail Club

COCKTAIL BAR

22 🍸 MAP P94, A7

There are cocktails and then there are cocktails. The guys in this slightly tatty ('kitsch punk') subterranean bar will shake, stir, blend and smoke (yes, smoke) you some of the most inventive, colourful and punchy concoctions in creation. Try the bacon and egg Martini or the smoked Manhattan. And relax. You might want to be here a while. (📞 020-7580 1960; www.londoncocktailclub.co.uk; 61 Goodge St, W1; ⏰ 4.30-11.30pm Mon-Thu, to midnight Fri & Sat; 🚇 Goodge St)

Princess Louise

PUB

23 🍺 MAP P94, E8

The ground-floor saloon of this pub dating from 1872 is spectacularly decorated with a riot of fine tiles, etched mirrors, plasterwork and a stunning central horseshoe bar. The old Victorian wood partitions give drinkers plenty of nooks and alcoves to hide in, and the frosted-glass 'snob screens' add further period allure. (📞 020-7405 8816; http://princesslouisepub.co.uk; 208 High Holborn, WC1; ⏰ 11am-11pm Mon-Fri, noon-11pm Sat, noon-6.45pm Sun; 🚇 Holborn)

Lamb

PUB

24 🍺 MAP P94, E5

The Lamb's central mahogany bar with beautiful Victorian 'snob screens' (so-called as they allowed the well-to-do to drink in private) has been a favourite with locals since 1729. Nearly three centuries later, its popularity hasn't waned, so come early to bag a booth and sample its good selection of Young's bitters and genial atmosphere. (📞 020-7405 0713; www.thelamblondon.com; 94 Lamb's Conduit St, WC1; ⏰ 11am-11pm Mon-Wed, to midnight Thu-Sat, noon-10.30pm Sun; 🚇 Russell Sq)

Entertainment

Scala

LIVE MUSIC

25 ⭐ MAP P94, E3

Opened in 1920 as a salubrious golden-age cinema, Scala slipped into porn-movie hell in the 1970s, only to be reborn as a club and live-music venue in the noughties. It's one of the best places in London to catch an intimate gig and is a great dance space too, hosting a diverse range of club nights. (📞 020-7833 2022; www.scala.co.uk; 275 Pentonville Rd, N1; 🚇 King's Cross St Pancras)

100 Club

LIVE MUSIC

26 ⭐ MAP P94, B8

This heritage London venue at the same address for over 75 years started off as a jazz club but now leans towards rock. Back in the day it showcased Chris Barber, BB King and the Rolling Stones, and it was at the centre of the punk revolution and the '90s indie scene. It hosts dancing gigs, the occasional big name, where-are-they-now bands and top-league

tributes. (☎020-7636 0933; www.
the100club.co.uk; 100 Oxford St, W1;
tickets £8-20; ◷check website for gig
times; ⊖Oxford Circus, Tottenham
Court Rd)

The Place DANCE

27 ⭐ MAP P94, C4

The birthplace of modern British
dance is one of London's most exciting cultural venues, still concen-
trating on challenging and experimental choreography. Behind the
late-Victorian terracotta facade
you'll find a 300-seat theatre, an
arty, creative cafe atmosphere and
a dozen training studios. Tickets
usually cost from £15. (☎020-7121
1100; www.theplace.org.uk; 17 Duke's
Rd, WC1; ⊖Euston Sq)

Shopping

James Smith & Sons FASHION & ACCESSORIES

28 🔒 MAP P94, C8

Nobody makes and stocks such
elegant umbrellas (not to mention walking sticks and canes) as
this place. It's been fighting the
British weather from the same
address since 1857 and, thanks to
London's ever-present downpours,
will hopefully do great business
for years to come. Prices start at
around £40 for a pocket umbrella.
(☎020-7836 4731; www.james-smith.
co.uk; 53 New Oxford St, WC1;
◷10am-5.45pm Mon, Tue, Thu & Fri,
10.30am-5.45pm Wed, 10am-5.15pm
Sat; ⊖Tottenham Court Rd)

James Smith & Sons

London Review Bookshop

BOOKS

29 🔒 MAP P94, D7

The flagship bookshop of the *London Review of Books* fortnightly literary journal doesn't put faith in towering piles of books and slabs on shelves, but offers a wide range of titles in a handful of copies only. It often hosts high-profile author talks (tickets usually £10), and there's a charming cafe where you can leaf through your new purchases. (📞020-7269 9030; www.londonreviewbookshop.co.uk; 14 Bury Pl, WC1; ⏱10am-6.30pm Mon-Sat, noon-6pm Sun; 🚇Holborn)

Fortnum & Mason

FOOD & DRINKS

30 🔒 MAP P94, C3

This small branch of the renowned department store, its first in more than 300 years, offers a good array of its signature teas (loose leaf or teabags) and coffees, which are great for last-minute presents and souvenirs if you're boarding a Eurostar. It also runs a cafe. (www.fortnumandmason.com; Unit 1a, St Pancras International Station, Pancras Rd, N1; ⏱7am-8pm Mon-Sat, 8am-8pm Sun; 🚇King's Cross St Pancras)

Forbidden Planet

COMICS

31 🔒 MAP P94, C8

Forbidden Planet is a trove of comics, sci-fi, horror and fantasy literature, as well as action figures and toys, spread over two floors. It's an absolute dream for anyone into manga comics, off-beat genre titles, and sci-fi and fantasy memorabilia. (📞020-7420 3666; www.forbiddenplanet.com; 179 Shaftesbury Ave, WC2; ⏱10am-7pm Mon & Tue, to 7.30pm Wed, Fri & Sat, to 8pm Thu, noon-6pm Sun; 🚇Tottenham Court Rd)

Gay's the Word

BOOKS

32 🔒 MAP P94, D5

This London gay institution has been selling books nobody else stocks since 1979, with a superb range of gay- and lesbian-interest books and magazines plus a real community spirit. Used books available as well. (📞020-7278 7654; www.gaystheword.co.uk; 66 Marchmont St, WC1; ⏱10am-6.30pm Mon-Sat, 2-6pm Sun; 🚇Russell Sq)

Folk

FASHION & ACCESSORIES

33 🔒 MAP P94, E6

Offers simple but strikingly styled casual clothes, often in bold colours and with a handcrafted feel. Head for No 49 for Folk's own line of menswear and to nearby No 53 for womenswear. (📞men's 020-7404 6458, women's 020-8616 4191; www.folkclothing.com; 49 Lamb's Conduit St, WC1; ⏱11am-7pm Mon-Fri, 10am-6pm Sat, noon-5pm Sun; 🚇Holborn)

Explore ◉
St Paul's
& the City

For its size, the City punches well above its weight for attractions, with an embarrassment of sightseeing riches. The heavyweights – the Tower of London and St Paul's – are a must, but combine the sights with exploration of the City's lesser-known delights, quieter corners and historic churches. The many churches make for peaceful stops along the way.

Make an early start to get ahead of the crowds besieging the Tower of London (p112). Explore Tower Bridge (p119) and have a table booked for lunch at Wine Library (p122). Head to St Paul's Cathedral (p108) and take a tour before making your way to the top of the staggering dome for choice views. If you've any time spare, explore the Museum of London (p118). To wind down, head for cocktails with views at Sky Pod (p123). Come back to earth for dinner at St John (p121) and round out the night in one of the City's historic pubs, such as Ye Olde Mitre (p123).

Getting There & Around
◉ The handiest stations are St Paul's (Central Line) and Bank (Central, Northern and Waterloo & City Lines, and DLR). Blackfriars (Circle and District Lines), Farringdon (Circle, Metropolitan and Hammersmith & City Lines) and Tower Hill (Circle and District Lines) are also useful.
🚌 Useful routes include 8, 15, 11 and 26.

St Paul's & the City Map on p116

Tower Bridge R.CLASSEN/SHUTTERSTOCK ©

Top Sight 📷
St Paul's Cathedral

Towering over diminutive Ludgate Hill in a position that's been a place of Christian worship for over 1400 years (and pagan before that), St Paul's is the City's most magnificent building. Built between 1675 and 1710 after the Great Fire destroyed its predecessor, Sir Christopher Wren's gleaming white-domed masterpiece became the very symbol of London's resistance and pride during WWII.

◉ **MAP P116, D4**

📞 020-7246 8357

www.stpauls.co.uk

St Paul's Churchyard, EC4

adult/child £18/8

🕑 8.30am-4.30pm
Mon-Sat

Ⓔ St Paul's

Dome

Wren wanted to construct a dome that was imposing on the outside but not overbearingly large on the inside. The solution was to build it in three parts: a plastered brick inner dome, a nonstructural lead outer dome and a brick cone between them holding it all together, one inside the other. This unique structure, second only in size to St Peter's in the Vatican, made the cathedral Wren's tour de force. Some 528 stairs take you to the top, but it's a three-stage journey.

Whispering Gallery

Enter through the door on the western side of the southern transept, where 257 steps lead to the interior walkway around the dome's base, 30m above the floor. This is the Whispering Gallery, so called because if you talk close to the wall it carries your words around to the opposite side, 32m away.

Stone Gallery & Golden Gallery

Climbing another 119 steps brings you to the Stone Gallery, an exterior viewing platform 53m above the ground, obscured by pillars and other suicide-preventing measures. The remaining 152 iron steps to the Golden Gallery are steeper and narrower than below but are really worth the effort. From here, 85m above London, you can enjoy superb 360-degree views of the city.

Interior

At a time of anti-Catholic fervour, it was controversial to build a Roman-style basilica rather than using the more familiar Gothic style. The interiors were more reflective of Protestant mores, though, being relatively unadorned, with large clear windows. The statues and mosaics that are now visible followed much later.

★ Top Tips

o There's no charge to attend a service. To hear the cathedral choir, attend Evensong (5pm Monday to Saturday and 3.15pm Sunday) or the 11.30am Sunday Eucharist.

o Admission includes a free audiovisual handset.

o Free 1½-hour guided tours depart four times daily (10am, 11am, 1pm and 2pm); reserve a place at the tour desk.

o Around twice a month, 60-minute tours (£8) also visit parts of the church that are usually off-limits; book ahead.

o Filming and photography is not permitted within the cathedral.

✗ Take a Break

In the crypt you'll find **Wren's Pantry** (www.searcysstpauls. co.uk; mains from £8; ◷ 9am-5pm), serving a selection of cakes, pastries and meals.

If you'd prefer not to eat in church, head to Miyama (p120) for delicious Japanese fare.

Duke of Wellington Memorial

In the north aisle of the vast nave you'll find the grandiose Duke of Wellington Memorial (1912), which took 54 years to complete – the Iron Duke's horse Copenhagen originally faced the other way, but it was deemed unfitting that a horse's rear end should face the altar. In contrast, just beneath the dome is an elegant epitaph written for Wren by his son: *Lector, si monumentum requiris, circumspice* (Reader, if you seek his monument, look around you).

The Light of the World & the Quire

In the north transept chapel is William Holman Hunt's celebrated painting, *The Light of the World* (1851–53), which depicts Christ knocking at a weed-covered door that, symbolically, can only be opened from within. Beyond, in the cathedral's heart, you'll find the spectacular Quire (or chancel) – its ceilings and arches dazzling with colourful mosaics – and the high altar. The ornately carved choir stalls by Dutch-British sculptor Grinling Gibbons on either side of the quire are exquisite, as are the ornamental wrought-iron gates, separating the aisles from the altar, by French Huguenot Jean Tijou.

American Memorial Chapel

Walk around the altar, with its massive gilded oak baldacchino

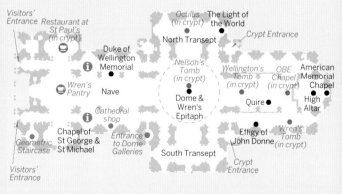

St Paul's Cathedral

Visitors' Entrance

Restaurant at St Paul's (in crypt)

Duke of Wellington Memorial

Wren's Pantry

Nave

Cathedral shop

Chapel of St George & St Michael

Geometric Staircase

Visitors' Entrance

Entrance to Dome Galleries

Oculus (in crypt)

The Light of the World

Crypt Entrance

North Transept

Nelson's Tomb (in crypt)

Wellington's Tomb (in crypt)

OBE Chapel (in crypt)

American Memorial Chapel

Dome & Wren's Epitaph

Quire

High Altar

South Transept

Effigy of John Donne

Wren's Tomb (in crypt)

Crypt Entrance

(canopy) with barley-twist columns, to the American Memorial Chapel, commemorating the 28,000 Americans based in Britain who lost their lives during WWII.

Crypt & the Oculus

On the eastern side of both the north and south transepts are stairs leading down to the crypt and the OBE Chapel, where services are held for members of the Order of the British Empire.

The crypt has memorials to around 300 of Britain's great and good, including Florence Nightingale, TE Lawrence (of Arabia) and Sir Winston Churchill. Those actually buried here include the Duke of Wellington, Vice Admiral Horatio Nelson, Sir Christopher Wren and the painters Sir Joshua Reynolds, Sir John Everett Millais, JMW Turner and William Holman Hunt.

The Oculus projects images onto the walls of the former treasury. If you're not up to climbing the dome, experience it here audiovisually.

Fifth Time Lucky

London's mother church has stood on this site since 604. Wren's cathedral is the fifth incarnation, built to replace the soaring Gothic-style Old St Paul's after it was destroyed in the Great Fire. The pre-Fire cathedral was both longer and taller than Wren's version.

Also in the crypt is the cathedral's **cafe** and **gift shop**.

Churchyard & Surrounds

Just outside the north transept, there's a simple, squat, round **monument to the people of London**, honouring the 32,000 civilians killed (and another 50,000 seriously injured) during WWII. Nearby is **St Paul's Cross**, topped by a gilded statue of the saint – an Edwardian replacement for the original preaching cross that was removed in 1643.

Top Sight 📷
Tower of London

With a history as bloody as it is fascinating, the Tower deserves to top the list of London sights. Begun during the reign of William the Conqueror, the Tower is in fact a castle containing 22 towers, and has served as a palace, an observatory, an armoury, a mint, a zoo, a prison and a site of execution.

◎ **MAP P116, H5**

www.hrp.org.uk/tower-of-london

Petty Wales, EC3

adult/child £24.80/11.50, audio guide £4/3

🕐 9am-4.30pm Tue-Sat, from 10am Sun-Mon

⊖ Tower Hill

Tower Green & Scaffold Site

What looks at first glance like a peaceful, almost village-like slice of the Tower's inner ward is actually one of its bloodiest. Those who have met their fate at the Scaffold Site include two of Henry VIII's wives, Anne Boleyn and Catherine Howard; 16-year-old Lady Jane Grey, who fell foul of Henry's daughter Mary I after her family attempted to have her crowned queen; and Robert Devereux, Earl of Essex, once a favourite of Elizabeth I. Just west of the scaffold site is **Beauchamp Tower** (1280), where high-ranking prisoners left behind unhappy inscriptions and other graffiti.

Chapel Royal of St Peter ad Vincula

On the northern edge of Tower Green is the 16th-century Chapel Royal of St Peter ad Vincula (St Peter in Chains), a rare surviving example of ecclesiastical Tudor architecture. Those buried here include three saints (Thomas More, John Fisher and Philip Howard, although the latter's body was subsequently moved to Arundel) and three queens (Anne Boleyn, Catherine Howard and Jane Grey). The church can be visited on a Yeoman Warder tour, or during the first and last hour of normal opening times.

Crown Jewels

To the east of the Chapel Royal and north of the White Tower is **Waterloo Barracks**, the home of the Crown Jewels. Once inside the vault, you'll be dazzled by lavishly bejewelled sceptres, orbs and, naturally, crowns. A moving walkway takes you past the dozen or so crowns and other coronation regalia, including the platinum crown of the late Queen Mother, Elizabeth, which is set with the 106-carat Koh-i-Nûr (Persian for 'Mountain of Light') diamond, and the State Sceptre with Cross topped with the 530-carat First Star of Africa (or Cullinan I)

★ Top Tips

○ Ticket sellers push the higher Gift Aid prices (which allows UK citizens to pass on a tax break to the Tower), but you shouldn't feel obliged to pay the additional £3.20.

○ Purchasing your ticket online (valid for seven days) will save a further £3.80 and avoid ticket queues.

○ Start with a free Yeoman Warder tour, which is a great way to familiarise yourself with the site.

○ Don't leave your visit until too late in the day, as there's lots to see.

✕ Take a Break

The red-brick **New Armouries Cafe** in the southeastern corner of the inner courtyard serves fish and chips, sandwiches and cakes.

If your explorations have worked up a thirst, the best pub nearby is the **Ship** (☏ 020-7702 4422; www.shipec3. co.uk; 3 Hart St, EC3; ⊙ 11.30am-11pm Mon-Fri; ⊖ Tower Hill).

diamond. A bit further on, exhibited on its own, is the centrepiece: the Imperial State Crown, set with 2868 diamonds (including the 317-carat Second Star of Africa, or Cullinan II), sapphires, emeralds, rubies and pearls. It's worn by the Queen at the State Opening of Parliament in May/June.

White Tower & the Royal Armouries

Built in stone as a fortress in 1078, this was the original 'Tower of London'; its name arose after Henry III whitewashed it in the 13th century. Not particularly tall by today's standards, in the Middle Ages it would have dwarfed the wooden huts surrounding the castle walls and intimidated the peasantry. Apart from **St John's Chapel**, most of its interior is given over to a Royal Armouries collection of cannons, guns and suits of mail and armour for men and horses. Among the most remarkable exhibits on the entrance floor are Henry VIII's two suits of armour, one made for him when he was a dashing 24-year-old and the other when he was a bloated 50-year-old with a waist measuring 129cm.

St John's Chapel

This unadorned chapel (1080), with its vaulted ceiling, rounded archways and 12 stone pillars, is a fine example of Norman architecture and the oldest place of Christian worship still standing in London.

Bloody Tower

The Bloody Tower (1225) takes its nickname from the 'princes in the tower', Edward V and his younger brother, held here and later murdered. Their uncle, Richard III, usually takes the blame, but you can vote for your prime suspect at an exhibition here. There are also exhibits on Elizabethan adventurer Sir Walter Raleigh, imprisoned here three times by Elizabeth I.

Medieval Palace

Inside **St Thomas' Tower**, discover what the hall and bedchamber of Edward I might once have looked like. Opposite St Thomas' Tower is **Wakefield Tower**, built by Henry III between 1220 and 1240 and now enticingly furnished with a replica throne and candelabra to give an impression of how it might have looked in Edward I's day.

Bowyer Tower

Behind the Waterloo Barracks is the Bowyer Tower, where George, Duke of Clarence, brother and rival of Edward IV, was imprisoned and, according to a long-standing legend that has never been proved, was drowned in a barrel of malmsey (sweet Madeira wine). The tower contains exhibits relating to the Duke of Wellington.

Wall Walk

The huge inner wall of the Tower was added in 1220 by Henry III. The Wall Walk takes in **Salt Tower**, **Broad**

Iconic Tower of London Sights

Yeoman Warders

A true icon of the Tower, the Yeoman Warders have been guarding the fortress since the 15th century. There can be up to 40 and, in order to qualify for the job, they must have served a minimum of 22 years in any branch of the British Armed Forces. In 2007 the first woman was appointed to the post. The Yeoman Warders may seem jovial, but don't go calling them Beefeaters – it's a nickname they're said to despise. The name has been around since at least the 17th century and its origins are unknown, although it's thought to be due to the rations of beef – then a luxury – given to them in the past. Lessening the offence somewhat, each warder receives a bottle of Beefeater Gin on their birthday as part of an old arrangement with its producers for use of their image on the bottle.

Ravens

Legend has it that Charles II requested that ravens always be kept at the Tower, as the kingdom would fall apart if they left. There are usually at least six ravens at the Tower and their wings are clipped to placate the superstitious.

Ceremony of the Keys

The elaborate locking of the main gates has been performed daily without fail for more than 700 years. The ceremony begins at 9.53pm precisely, and it's all over by 10.05pm. Even when a bomb hit the Tower of London during the Blitz, the ceremony was only delayed by 30 minutes – some say that displays the essence of the famed British stiff upper lip, others their sheer lunacy. Entry to the ceremony begins at 9.30pm and is free, but you must book in advance online (www.hrp.org.uk).

Arrow and **Constable Towers** and ends with **Martin Tower**, housing an exhibition of original coronation regalia. Colonel Thomas Blood, disguised as a clergyman, attempted to steal the Crown Jewels from here in 1671.

Tours

While they officially guard the Tower, the Yeoman Warder's main role these days is as tour guides. Free hour-long **tours** leave from the Middle Tower every 30 minutes until 3.30pm (2.30pm in winter).

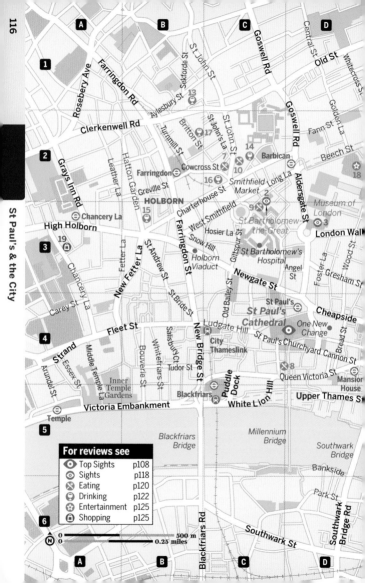

St Paul's & the City

A
B
C
D

1
2
3
4
5
6

Rosebery Ave
Farringdon Rd
Clerkenwell Rd
Grays Inn Rd
Leather La
Hatton Garden
Greville St
Sekforde St
St John St
Aylesbury St
Turnmill St
Britton St
St John's La
St John St
Cowcross St
Charterhouse St
West Smithfield
Snow Hill
Holborn Viaduct
Newgate St
Old Bailey
Goswell Rd
Goswell Rd
Central St
Old St
Whitecross St
Fann St
Golden La
Beech St
Aldersgate St
Long La
Gresham St
Foster La
Wood St
Cheapside
Bread St
Cannon St

HOLBORN
Farringdon ⊖
Chancery La ⊖
High Holborn
Fetter La
St Andrew St
New Fetter La
Chancery La
Carey St
Fleet St
Salisbury Ct
Whitefriars St
Bouverie St
Tudor St
Strand
Essex St
Arundel St
Middle Temple
Temple ⊖
Inner Temple Gardens
Victoria Embankment
New Bridge St
Blackfriars ⊖
Puddle Dock
White Lion Hill
City Thameslink

13
17
14
10
Barbican
18
Smithfield Market
16
15
2
9
St Bartholomew-the-Great
St Bartholomew's Hospital
Angel St
London Wall
Museum of London
3
19
St Paul's Cathedral
St Paul's ⊖
One New Change
St Paul's Churchyard
8
Queen Victoria St
Mansion House ⊖
Upper Thames St

Beech St
18 ☆

Ludgate Hill

Blackfriars Bridge
Millennium Bridge
Southwark Bridge
Bankside
Park St
Southwark St
Blackfriars Rd
Southwark Bridge Rd

Gittspur St
Hosier La

For reviews see
⊙ Top Sights	p108
⊙ Sights	p118
⊗ Eating	p120
⊙ Drinking	p122
☆ Entertainment	p125
🔒 Shopping	p125

500 m
0.25 miles
N

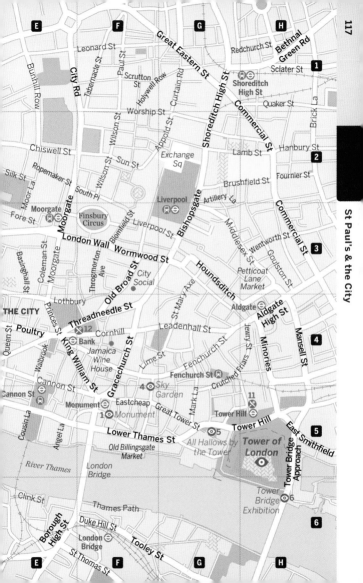

E **F** **G** **H**

Redchurch St

Bethnal
Great Eastern St   Green Rd

Leonard St   Sclater St   **1**

City Rd   Paul St   Scrutton St   Shoreditch High St   Shoreditch
                                                                                 High St   Quaker St   Brick La

Tabernacle St   Holywell Row   Curtain Rd   Commercial St

Worship St   Hanbury St   **2**

Chiswell St   Appold St   Lamb St   Fournier St

Wilson St   Sun St   Exchange Sq   Brushfield St

Ropemaker St   South Pl   Artillery La   Commercial St

Silk St   Wilson St   Liverpool   Bishopsgate   **3**

Fore St   Moorgate   Liverpool St   Middlesex St   Wentworth St   Goulston St

Moor La   Finsbury Circus   Blomfield St   Petticoat
Basinghall St   Moorgate   Lane Market

London Wall   Wormwood St   Houndsditch   Aldgate   Aldgate High St   Mansell St

Throgmorton Ave   Old Broad St   St Mary Axe   **4**

THE CITY   Lothbury   City Social   Leadenhall St

Poultry   Threadneedle St ✕12   Cornhill   Lime St   Fenchurch St   Jewry St   Minories

Princes St   Bank   Jamaica Wine House   Crutched Friars

Queen St   Walbrook   King William St   Gracechurch St   Fenchurch St 🚉

Cannon St   Cannon St   4 ◉ Sky Garden   11 ✕

Monument 🚇   Eastcheap   Great Tower St   Tower Hill 🚇   **5**
1 ◉ Monument
Cousin La   Angel La   Lower Thames St   5   Tower Hill   East Smithfield

River Thames   Old Billingsgate Market   All Hallows by the Tower   Tower of London   Tower Bridge Approach

London Bridge

Clink St   Tower Bridge Exhibition   6 ◉   **6**

Borough High St   Thames Path   London Bridge 🚇   Duke Hill St

Tooley St   St Thomas St

E **F** **G** **H**

Sights

Monument

TOWER

1 ◉ MAP P116, F5

Sir Christopher Wren's 1677 column, known simply as the Monument, is a memorial to the Great Fire of London of 1666, whose impact on London's history cannot be overstated. An immense Doric column made of Portland stone, the Monument is 4.5m wide and 60.6m tall – the exact distance it stands from the bakery in Pudding Lane where the fire is thought to have started. Note, tickets can only be purchased with cash. (☏020-7403 3761; www.themonument.org.uk; Fish St Hill, EC3; adult/child £5/2.50, incl Tower Bridge Exhibition £12/5.50; ⏰9.30am-5.30pm Apr-Sep, to 5pm Oct-Mar; ⊖Monument)

St Bartholomew-the-Great

CHURCH

2 ◉ MAP P116, C2

Dating to 1123 and adjoining one of London's oldest hospitals, St Bartholomew-the-Great is one of London's most ancient churches. The Norman arches and profound sense of history lend this holy space an ancient calm, while approaching from nearby Smithfield Market through the restored 13th-century half-timbered archway is like walking back in time. The church was originally part of an Augustinian priory; but became the parish church of Smithfield in 1539 when Henry VIII dissolved the monasteries. (☏020-7600 0440; www.greatstbarts.com; West Smithfield, EC1; adult/child £5/3; ⏰8.30am-5pm Mon-Fri, 10.30am-4pm Sat, 8.30am-8pm Sun; ⊖Barbican)

Museum of London

MUSEUM

3 ◉ MAP P116, D3

As entertaining as it is educational, the Museum of London meanders through the various incarnations of the city, stopping off in Roman Londinium and Saxon Ludenwic before eventually ending up in the 21st-century metropolis. Interesting objects and interactive displays work together to bring each era to life, without ever getting too whizz-bang, making this one of the capital's best museums. Free themed tours take place throughout the day; check the signs by the entrance for times. (☏020-7001 9844; www.museumoflondon.org.uk; 150 London Wall, EC2; admission free; ⏰10am-6pm; ⊖Barbican)

Sky Garden

VIEWPOINT

4 ◉ MAP P116, F5

The City's sixth-tallest building didn't get off to a good start when it opened in 2014. Officially called 20 Fenchurch St it was quickly dubbed the 'Walkie Talkie' by unimpressed Londoners, and its highly reflective windows melted the bodywork of several cars parked below. However, the opening of this 155m-high, three-storey, public garden in the glass dome at the top has helped win naysayers over.

Entry is free, but you'll need to book a slot in advance. (📞020-7337 2344; www.skygarden.london; L35-37, 20 Fenchurch St, EC3; admission free; 🕙10am-6pm Mon-Fri, 11am-9pm Sat & Sun; 🚇Monument)

All Hallows by the Tower
CHURCH

5 ◎ MAP P116, G5

All Hallows (meaning 'all saints'), which dates from AD 675, survived virtually unscathed the Great Fire, only to be hit by German bombs in 1940. Come to see the church itself, by all means, but the best bits are in the atmospheric undercroft (crypt), where you'll discover a pavement of 2nd-century Roman tiles and the walls of the 7th-century Saxon church.

Free 20-minute tours are available between 2pm and 4pm most weekdays from April to October. (📞020-7481 2928; www.ahbtt.org.uk; Byward St, EC3; 🕙8am-6pm Mon-Fri, 10am-5pm Sat & Sun Apr-Oct, 8am-5pm Mon-Fri, 10am-5pm Sat & Sun Nov-Mar; 🚇Tower Hill)

Tower Bridge Exhibition
BRIDGE

6 ◎ MAP P116, H6

This fascinating exhibition explains the nuts and bolts of Tower Bridge. If you're not technically minded, it's still fascinating to get inside the bridge and look along the Thames from its two walkways. A lift takes you to the top, 42m above the river, where you can walk along each of the walkways, which are

Sky Garden

lined with information boards. A wow-inducing 11m-long glass floor provides views plunging to the road and river below. (☎020-7403 3761; www.towerbridge.org.uk; Tower Bridge, SE1; adult/child £9.80/4.20, incl the Monument £12/5.50; ⊗10am-5.30pm Apr-Sep, 9.30am-5pm Oct-Mar; ⊖Tower Hill)

Eating

Polpo ITALIAN £

7 ⊗ MAP P116, C2

Occupying a sunny spot on semipedestrianised Cowcross St, this sweet little place serves rustic Venetian-style meatballs, *pizzette* (small pizzas), grilled meat and fish dishes. Portions are larger than your average tapas but a tad smaller than a regular main – the perfect excuse to sample more than one of the exquisite dishes. Exceptional value for money. (☎020-7250 0034; www.polpo.co.uk; 3 Cowcross St, EC1M; dishes £4-12; ⊗11.30am-11pm Mon-Thu & Sat, to midnight Fri, to 4pm Sun; ⊖Farringdon)

Miyama JAPANESE ££

8 ⊗ MAP P116, C4

There's the sense of a well-kept secret about this friendly Japanese restaurant, tucked away in a basement of a nondescript building (enter from Knightrider St). Miyama offers something for everyone, from soba and udon noodles to sushi and bento boxes. Sit at the sushi or teppanyaki bar for culinary drama, or opt for the more discreet main restaurant.

Polpo

The Great Fire of London

With nearly all its buildings constructed from wood, for centuries London had been prone to conflagration, but it wasn't until 2 September 1666 that the mother of all blazes broke out, in a bakery in Pudding Lane in the City. It didn't seem like much to begin with – the mayor himself dismissed it as being easily extinguished, before going back to bed – but the unusual September heat combined with rising winds to spark a tinderbox effect. The fire raged out of control for days, reducing around 80% of London to carbon. Only eight people died (officially at least), but most of London's medieval, Tudor and Jacobean architecture was destroyed.

The fire was finally stopped (at Fetter Lane, on the very edge of London) by blowing up all the buildings in the inferno's path. It's hard to overstate the scale of the destruction – 89 churches and more than 13,000 houses were razed, leaving tens of thousands of people homeless. Many Londoners left for the countryside or sought their fortunes in the New World.

(020-7489 1937; www.miyama-restaurant.co.uk; 17 Godliman St, EC4; mains £8-26; 11.30am-2.30pm & 5.45- 9.30pm Mon-Fri; St Paul's)

Club Gascon
FRENCH ££

9 MAP P116, C3

Marble walls, white linen and exceedingly professional staff lend an old-fashioned gentlemen's-club feel to this Michelin-starred restaurant. Dishes from France's southwest are given a contemporary work over and while it's not cheap, Gascon does offer an excellent two-course 'express lunch' (£25). Don't be shy about requesting the 'express' menu as it's not always proffered automatically. (020-7600 6144; www.clubgascon.com; 57 West Smithfield, EC1; mains £16-28; noon-2pm &

6-10pm Tue-Fri, 6-10pm Sat; Barbican)

St John
BRITISH ££

10 MAP P116, C2

Whitewashed brick walls, high ceilings and simple wooden furniture don't make for a cosy dining space but they do keep diners free to concentrate on St John's famous nose-to-tail dishes. Serves are big, hearty and a celebration of England's culinary past. Don't miss the signature roast bone marrow and parsley salad (£8.90). (020-7251 0848; www.stjohngroup.uk.com/spitalfields; 26 St John St, EC1M; mains £14.80-24.90; noon-3pm & 6-11pm Mon-Fri, 6-11pm Sat, 12.30-4pm Sun; Farringdon)

Free View over London

Designed by Jean Nouvel, **One New Change** (Map p116, D4; www. onenewchange.com; 1 New Change, EC4M; ⊙10am-6pm Mon-Wed & Sat, 10am-8pm Thu & Fri, noon-6pm Sun; ⊖St Paul's) – called the 'Stealth Bomber' by some because of its distinctive shape – is a shopping mall housing mainly high-street brands, but take the lift to its 6th floor and an open viewing platform will reward you with up-close views of the dome of St Paul's Cathedral and out over London.

Wine Library   BUFFET ££

11 ✖ MAP P116, H5

This is a great place for a light but boozy lunch opposite the Tower. Buy a bottle of wine at retail price from the large selection (£9.50 corkage fee) and then head into the vaulted cellar to snack as much as you like from the selection of delicious pâtés, charcuterie, cheeses, bread and salads. (☏020-7481 0415; www.winelibrary.co.uk; 43 Trinity Sq, EC3; buffet £18; ⊙buffet 11.30am-3.30pm, shop 10am-6pm Mon, to 8pm Tue-Fri; ⊖Tower Hill)

Sauterelle   EUROPEAN £££

12 ✖ MAP P116, F4

Take a seat on the elegant mezzanine of the **Royal Exchange** (☏020-7283 8935; www.theroyalexchange.co.uk) and prepare to be pampered with professional service and a menu of sophisticated British, French and Italian fare. Prices befit the sumptuous surroundings, but the restaurant also offers an excellent-value set menu (two/three courses £20/25), although you may need to ask to be shown it. (☏020-7618 2480; www.royalexchange-grandcafe.co.uk; Threadneedle St, EC3; mains £26-30; ⊙noon-11pm Mon-Fri; ⊖Bank)

Drinking

Zetter Townhouse Cocktail Lounge   COCKTAIL BAR

13 ⬤ MAP P116, B1

Tucked away behind an unassuming door on St John's Sq, this ground-floor bar is decorated with plush armchairs, stuffed animal heads and a legion of lamps. The cocktail list takes its theme from the area's distilling history – recipes of yesteryear plus homemade tinctures and cordials are used to create interesting and unusual tipples. House cocktails are all £11. (☏020-7324 4545; www. thezettertownhouse.com; 49-50 St John's Sq, EC1V; ⊙7.30am-12.45am; ���; ⊖Farringdon)

Fox & Anchor PUB

14 MAP P116, C2

Behind the Fox & Anchor's wonderful art nouveau facade is a stunning traditional Victorian pub that has retained its three beautiful snugs at the back of the bar. Fully celebrating its proximity to Smithfield Market, the food is gloriously meaty. Only the most voracious of carnivores should opt for the City Boy Breakfast (£19.50). (www.foxandanchor.com; 115 Charterhouse St, EC1M; ⏱7am-11pm Mon-Fri, 8.30am-11pm Sat & Sun; 🛜; ⊖Barbican)

Ye Olde Mitre PUB

15 MAP P116, B3

A delightfully cosy historic pub with an extensive beer selection, tucked away in a backstreet off Hatton Garden, Ye Olde Mitre was built in 1546 for the servants of Ely Palace. There's no music, so rooms echo only with amiable chit-chat. Queen Elizabeth I danced around the cherry tree by the bar, they say. (www.yeoldemitreholborn.co.uk; 1 Ely Ct, EC1N; ⏱11am-11pm Mon-Fri; 🛜; ⊖Farringdon)

Sky Pod BAR

You'll need a booking for the Sky Garden (p118) to access this rooftop bar (see 4 Map p116, F5), and if you'd like a guaranteed table to sit at, you're best to book one at the same time. The views are extraordinary, although it does get cold up here in winter. Note, it doesn't accept shorts, sportswear, trainers or flip-flops after 5pm.

Fox & Anchor

Top Spots in the City for...

Culture vulture nest A powerhouse of culture (though not the prettiest kid in class), people flock to the **Barbican** for its innovative dance, theatre, music, films and art.

Meals with a view There's nothing like getting a taste of the high life, trying to spot your hotel and watching the sun go down over the capital at Tower 42's **City Social** (Map p116, F3; ☑ 020-7877 7703; www.citysociallondon.com; L24, 25 Old Broad St, EC2; mains £26-38; ☺ noon-3.30pm & 6-11.30pm Mon-Fri, 5-11.30pm Sat; ☻ Bank).

Old-style drinking Though they tend to keep bankers' hours, the City's pubs are some of the most atmospheric and historic – the **Jamaica Wine House** (Map p116, F4; ☑ 020-7929 6972; www. jamaicawinehouse.co.uk; 12 St Michael's Alley, EC3; ☺ 11am-11pm Mon-Fri; ☻ Bank) once did time as London's first coffee house.

(☑ 0333 772 0020; www.skygarden. london; L35, 20 Fenchurch St, EC3; ☺ 7am-11pm Mon, to midnight Tue, to 1am Wed-Fri, 8am-1am Sat, 8am-11pm Sun; ☻ Monument)

Fabric
CLUB

16 ☻ MAP P116, C2

London's leading club, Fabric's three separate dance floors in a huge converted cold store opposite Smithfield meat market draws impressive queues (buy tickets online). FabricLive (on selected Fridays) rumbles with drum 'n' bass and dubstep, while Fabric (usually on Saturdays but also on selected Fridays) is the club's signature live DJ night. Sunday's WetYourSelf! delivers house, techno and electronica. (☑ 0207 336 8898; www.fabric

london.com; 77a Charterhouse St, EC1M; cover £5-25; ☺ 11pm-7am Fri, to 8am Sat, to 5.30am Sun; ☻ Farringdon, Barbican)

Jerusalem Tavern
PUB

17 ☻ MAP P116, B2

Pick a wood-panelled cubicle at this tiny and highly atmospheric pub housed in a building dating from 1720 and select from the fantastic beverages brewed by St Peter's Brewery in Suffolk. Be warned: it's hugely popular and often very crowded. (www. stpetersbrewery.co.uk; 55 Britton St, EC1M; ☺ 11am-11pm Mon-Fri; ☎; ☻ Farringdon)

Entertainment

Barbican Centre

PERFORMING ARTS

18 ⭐ MAP P116, D2

Home to the London Symphony Orchestra and the BBC Symphony Orchestra, the **Barbican** (📞020-7638 4141; tours adult/child £12.50/10; 🕐9am-11pm Mon-Sat, 11am-11pm Sun) also hosts scores of other concerts, focusing in particular on jazz, folk, world and soul artists. Dance is also performed here, while the cinema screens recent releases as well as film festivals. (📞020-7638 8891; www.barbican. org.uk; Silk St, EC2; 🕐box office 10am-8pm Mon-Sat, 11am-8pm Sun; ⊖Barbican)

Shopping

London Silver Vaults

ARTS & CRAFTS

19 🔒 MAP P116, A3

The 30-odd shops that work out of these secure subterranean vaults make up the largest collection of silver under one roof in the world. The different businesses tend to specialise in particular types of silverware – from cutlery sets to picture frames, animal sculptures and lots of jewellery. (📞020-7242 3844; www.silvervault-slondon.com; 53-63 Chancery Lane, WC2; 🕐9am-5.30pm Mon-Fri, to 1pm Sat; ⊖Chancery Lane)

Walking Tour 🚶

An Olympic Stroll in East London

The 2012 Olympic Games succeeded in transforming great stretches of East London. Around the stadium itself, what was once a vast brownfield site is now a flourishing park with leading sports venues, wetlands and even an urban beach. The regeneration has spread to surrounding neighbourhoods such as Hackney Wick and helped turn unsung areas around Victoria Park into desirable real estate.

Getting There

🚇 Stratford is on the Central and Jubilee Lines. Bethnal Green is on the Central Line.

🚃 Stratford is on the Overground.

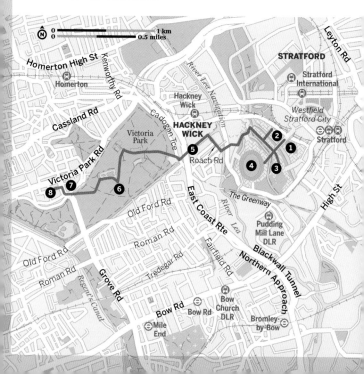

❶ Aquatics Centre

The sweeping lines and wave-like movement of Zaha Hadid's award-winning London **Aquatics Centre** (www.londonaquaticscentre.org; adult/child from £5.20/3; ⏱6am-10.30pm) make it the architectural highlight of Queen Elizabeth Olympic Park. Bathed in natural light, the 50m competition pool lies beneath a huge undulating roof which sits on just three supports.

❷ Boat Tour on the Lea

The Olympic Park (and its numerous venues) stretches over several hectares along the River Lea, so a good way to take it all in is to join a **Lee & Stort Boats** (www.leeandstortboats.co.uk; Stratford waterfront pontoon, E20; adult/child £9/4; ⏱daily Apr-Sep, Sat & Sun Mar & Oct) tour.

❸ ArcelorMittal Orbit

At 115m in height, this distinctive twisted steel **structure** (www.arcelormittalorbit.com; 3 Thornton St, E20; adult/child £12.50/7.50, with slide £17.50/12.50; ⏱11am-5pm Mon-Fri, 10am-6pm Sat & Sun) by Turner Prize–winner Anish Kapoor offers a fantastic panorama from its viewing platform.

❹ London Stadium

The centrepiece of Olympic Park, 54,000-seat **London Stadium** (www.london-stadium.com; tours adult/child £19/11; ⏱tours 10am-4.15pm) is now the home ground for West Ham United FC. When no sporting events or concerts are on, self-guided multimedia tours are available.

❺ Hackney Wick & Hertford Union Canal

Across the canal from Olympic Park, Hackney Wick has become an artsy enclave over recent years. Former warehouses have been emblazoned with graffiti and converted into flats, studios and microbrewery bars, such as the excellent **Howling Hops** (www.howlinghops.co.uk; ⏱noon-11pm Sun-Thu, to midnight Fri & Sat).

❻ Victoria Park

The 'Regent's Park of the East End', **Victoria Park** (www.towerhamlets.gov.uk/victoriapark; ⏱7am-dusk) is an 86-hectare leafy expanse of ornamental lakes, monuments, tennis courts, flower beds and large lawns. When it opened in 1845 it was the first public park in the East End.

❼ Royal Inn on the Park

On the northern border of Victoria Park, this excellent **pub** (www.royalinnonthepark.com; ⏱noon-11pm; 📶) has real ales and Czech lagers on tap, outside seating to the front and a large courtyard at the back. It's always lively and attracts a mixed crowd.

❽ Dinner at Empress

End your East London meander with dinner at **Empress** (www.empresse9.co.uk; mains £13.50-18.50; ⏱6-10.15pm Mon, noon-3.30pm & 6-10.15pm Tue-Sat, 10am-9.30pm Sun). An upmarket gastropub, it serves fantastic modern British cuisine, with a drinks selection to match.

Explore ✦

Tate Modern & South Bank

The South Bank has transformed from an ill-loved backwater into one of London's must-see areas. A roll call of riverside sights lines the Thames, beginning with the London Eye, running past the cultural enclave of the Southbank Centre and on to the outstanding Tate Modern, Millennium Bridge, Shakespeare's Globe, waterside pubs, a cathedral and one of London's most-visited food markets.

Pre-booked ticket for the London Eye (p136) in hand, enjoy a leisurely revolution in the skies for astronomical city views (if the weather's clear). Hop on a bus to the Imperial War Museum (p137), where trench warfare, the Holocaust and London during the Blitz are brilliantly documented. Stop at the Anchor & Hope (p141) for lunch before making your way to the Tate Modern (p130). Raise a cocktail to the staggering views over the Thames at Oblix (p142) before devouring exquisite mezzes at Arabica Bar & Kitchen (p142). Theatre lovers should have tickets booked for the National Theatre (p144) or the Old Vic (p144).

Getting There & Around

🚇 Waterloo, Southwark and London Bridge are on the Jubilee Line. London Bridge and Waterloo are also served by the Northern Line (and National Rail).
🚌 The Riverside RV1 runs around the South Bank and Bankside, linking all the main sights.

South Bank Map on p134

Top Sight 📷
Tate Modern

One of London's most amazing attractions, this outstanding modern- and contemporary-art gallery is housed in the creatively revamped Bankside Power Station. A spellbinding synthesis of modern art and capacious industrial brick design, Tate Modern has been extraordinarily successful in bringing challenging work to the masses, both through its free permanent collection and fee-paying big-name temporary exhibitions.

◉ MAP P134, E2

www.tate.org.uk

admission free

🕙 10am-6pm Sun-Thu, to 10pm Fri & Sat

⊖ Blackfriars, Southwark, London Bridge

Boiler House

The original gallery lies in what was once Bankside Power Station. Now called Boiler House, it is an imposing sight: a 200m-long building, made of 4.2 million bricks. Its conversion into an art gallery was a master stroke of design: the 'Tate Modern effect' is clearly as much about the building and its location (cue the ever popular balconies on level 3 with their magnificent views of St Paul's) as it is about the mostly 20th-century art inside.

Turbine Hall

The first thing to greet you as you pour down the ramp off Holland St at the main entrance is the astounding 3300-sq-metre Turbine Hall. Originally housing the power station's humungous electricity generators, this vast space has become the commanding venue for large-scale installation art and temporary exhibitions. Some art critics swipe at its populism, particularly the 'participatory art' (Carsten Höller's funfair-like slides Test Site; Doris Salcedo's enormous Shibboleth fissure in the floor; and Robert Morris' climbable geometric sculpture), but others insist this makes art more accessible. Note, if you enter instead from the river entrance, you'll end up on the more-muted level 1.

Permanent Collection

Tate Modern's permanent collection is arranged by both theme and chronology on levels 2 and 4 of Boiler House and levels 0, 2, 3 and 4 of Switch House. The emphasis in the latter is on art from the 1960s onwards.

More than 60,000 works are on constant rotation, which can be frustrating if you'd like to see one particular piece, but keeps it thrilling for repeat visitors. Helpfully, you can check the excellent website to see whether a specific work is on display – and where.

★ Top Tips

o Audio guides (in five languages) are available for £4. They contain explanations about 50 artworks across the galleries and offer suggested tours for adults or children.

o Free guided highlights tours depart at 11am, noon, 2pm and 3pm daily.

o Boiler House and Switch House are connected at levels 0, 1 and 4; get yourself a map (£1) to make navigating easier.

✗ Take a Break

If you've worked up an appetite while traipsing from Boiler House to Switch House, head to gastropub Anchor & Hope (p141) for fine Modern British fare.

For highly original cocktails and a little pizzazz, try **Dandelyan** (www. mondrianlondon.com; Mondrian London, 20 Upper Ground, SE1; 4pm-1am Mon-Wed, noon-2am Thu-Sat, to 12.30am Sun; Southwark).

The curators have at their disposal paintings by Georges Braque, Henri Matisse, Piet Mondrian, Andy Warhol, Mark Rothko and Jackson Pollock, as well as pieces by Joseph Beuys, Damien Hirst, Rebecca Horn, Claes Oldenburg and Auguste Rodin.

A great place to begin is the Start Display on level 2 of Boiler House: this small, specially curated 'taster' display features some of the best-loved works in the collection and gives visitors useful pointers for how to go about tackling unfamiliar (and an overwhelming amount of) art.

Switch House

The new Tate Modern extension takes its name from the former electrical substation that still occupies the southeast end of the site. To echo its sister building, it is also constructed of brick, although here these are slightly lighter and have been artistically laid out in a lattice to let light in (and out – the building looks stunning after dark).

The interior is rather stark, with raw, unpolished concrete (the original look of the Tanks) vaguely reminiscent of decrepit brutalist buildings, but the exhibition space is fantastic, giving the collection the room it deserves to breathe and shine.

The Tanks

The three huge subterranean tanks once stored fuel for the

Tate of the Art

Swiss architects Herzog & de Meuron scooped the prestigious Pritzker Architecture Prize for their transformation of empty Bankside Power Station, which closed in 1981. Leaving the building's single central 99m-high chimney, adding a two-storey glass box onto the roof and employing the cavernous Turbine Hall as a dramatic entrance space were three strokes of genius. Herzog & de Meuron also designed the new Tate extension, Switch House.

power station. These unusual circular spaces are now dedicated to showing live art, performance, installation and film, or 'new art' as the Tate calls it.

Special Exhibitions

With the opening of Switch House, the Tate Modern has increased the number of special exhibitions it hosts. You will find the exhibits on levels 3 and 4 of Boiler House and level 2 of Switch House; all are subject to admission charges (adult tickets cost £12.50 to £18.50; children enter free).

Past special exhibitions have included retrospectives on Henri Matisse, Edward Hopper, Frida Kahlo, Roy Lichtenstein, August Strindberg, Nazism and 'Degenerate' Art, Joan Miró and Amedeo Modigliani.

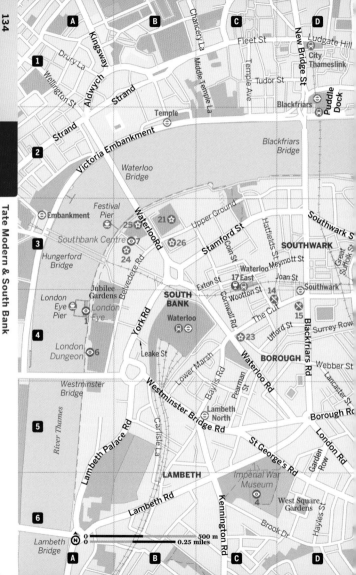

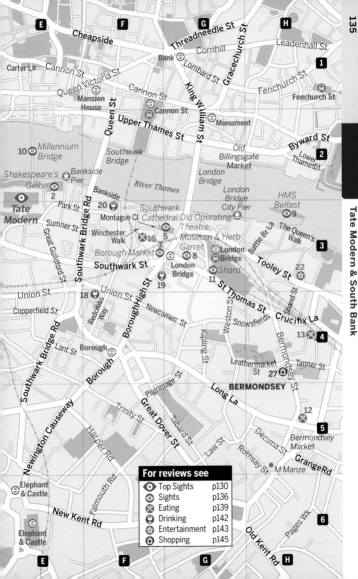

Tate Modern & South Bank

E **F** **G** **H**

Cheapside

Threadneedle St

Cornhill

Leadenhall St

1

Carter La Cannon St

Queen Victoria St

Bank

Lombard St

Gracechurch St

Fenchurch St

Cannon St

Cannon St

Mansion House

Queen St

Upper Thames St

King William St

Cannon St

Monument

Fenchurch St

Byward St

Lower Thames St

2

10 Millennium Bridge

Southwark Bridge

Old Billingsgate Market

Shakespeare's Globe

Bankside Pier

Bankside

River Thames

London Bridge

London Bridge City Pier

HMS Belfast

9

2

Tate Modern

Park St

20

Montague Cl

Southwark Bridge Rd

Southwark Cathedral

Old Operating Theatre

The Queen's Walk

3

Sumner St

Winchester Walk

16

5

Museum & Herb Garret

Battle Br La

Great Guildford St

Borough Market

3

8

London Bridge

Tooley St

22

Southwark St

London Bridge

Shard

St Thomas St

Crucifix La

13

4

19

11

Union St

18

Union St

Borough High St

Newcomen St

Weston St

Snowsfields

Bermondsey St

Copperfield St

Redcross Way

Kipling St

Leathermarket St

Tanner St

27

BERMONDSEY

Southwark Bridge Rd

Lant St

Borough

Borough

Pilgrimage St

Long La

12

Newington Causeway

Great Dover St

Trinity St

Tabard St

Decima St

Bermondsey Market

5

Harper Rd

Falmouth Rd

Law St

Rothsay St

Grange Rd

M Manze

Elephant & Castle

For reviews see

Elephant & Castle

New Kent Rd

Old Kent Rd

Pages Wlk

6

For reviews see	
⊙ Top Sights	p130
⊙ Sights	p136
⊗ Eating	p139
⊗ Drinking	p142
☆ Entertainment	p143
⊕ Shopping	p145

E **F** **G** **H**

Sights

London Eye
VIEWPOINT

1 ⊙ MAP P134, A4

Standing 135m high in a fairly flat city, the London Eye affords views 25 miles in every direction, weather permitting. Interactive tablets provide great information (in six languages) about landmarks as they appear in the skyline. Each rotation – or 'flight' – takes a gracefully slow 30 minutes. At peak times (July, August and school holidays) it can feel like you'll spend more time in the queue than in the capsule; book premium fast-track tickets to jump the queue. (📞0871 222 4002; www.londoneye.com; adult/child £27/22; ⏰11am-6pm Sep-May, 10am-8.30pm Jun-Aug; 🚇Waterloo, Westminster)

Shakespeare's Globe
HISTORIC BUILDING

2 ⊙ MAP P134, E2

Unlike other venues for Shakespearean plays, the new Globe was designed to resemble the original as closely as possible, which means having the arena open to the fickle London skies, leaving the 700 'groundlings' (standing spectators) to weather London's spectacular downpours. Visits to the Globe include tours of the theatre (half-hourly) as well as access to the exhibition space, which has fascinating exhibits on Shakespeare and theatre in the 17th century. (📞020-7902 1500; www.shakespearesglobe.com; 21 New Globe Walk, SE1; adult/child £17/10; ⏰9.30am-5pm; 🚻; 🚇Blackfriars, London Bridge)

Borough Market
MARKET

3 ⊙ MAP P134, F3

Located in this spot in some form or another since the 13th century (possibly since 1014), 'London's Larder' has enjoyed an astonishing renaissance in the past 15 years. Always overflowing with food lovers, inveterate gastronomes, wide-eyed visitors and Londoners in search of inspiration for their dinner party, this fantastic market has become firmly established as a sight in its own right. The market specialises in high-end fresh

---

The South Bank

The South Bank can be split into three main 'hubs' for sights: the area right on its southwestern fringe, where the London Eye and Southbank Centre are located; the area known as 'Bankside', where you'll find the Tate Modern, Shakespeare's Globe Theatre and Borough Market; and finally the stretch between London Bridge and Tower Bridge, where landmarks such as the Shard, HMS *Belfast* and City Hall congregate.

products; there are also plenty of takeaway stalls and an almost unreasonable number of cake stalls. (www.boroughmarket.org.uk; 8 Southwark St, SE1; ⏱10am-5pm Wed & Thu, 10am-6pm Fri, 8am-5pm Sat; 🚇London Bridge)

Imperial War Museum

MUSEUM

4 ◉ MAP P134, C6

Fronted by a pair of intimidating 15in naval guns, this riveting museum is housed in what was the Bethlehem Royal Hospital, a psychiatric hospital also known as Bedlam. Although the museum's focus is on military action involving British or Commonwealth troops largely during the 20th century, it rolls out the carpet to war in the wider sense. Highlights include the state-of-the-art **First World War Galleries** and **Witnesses to War** in the forecourt and atrium above. (📞020-7416 5000; www.iwm.org. uk; Lambeth Rd, SE1; admission free; ⏱10am-6pm; 🚇Lambeth North)

Southwark Cathedral

CHURCH

5 ◉ MAP P134, G3

The earliest surviving parts of this relatively small cathedral are the retrochoir at the eastern end, which contains four chapels and was part of the 13th-century Priory of St Mary Overie, some ancient arcading by the southwest door and an arch that dates to the original Norman church. But most of the cathedral is Victorian. In-

side there are monuments galore, including a Shakespeare memorial. Catch evensong at 5.30pm on four weekdays a week, 4pm on Saturdays and 3pm on Sundays. (📞020-7367 6700; www.cathedral. southwark.anglican.org; Montague Cl, SE1; ⏱8am-6pm Mon-Fri, 8.30am-6pm Sat & Sun; 🚇London Bridge)

London Dungeon

HISTORIC BUILDING

6 ◉ MAP P134, A4

Older kids tend to love the London Dungeon, as the terrifying queues during school holidays and weekends testify. It's all spooky music, ghostly boat rides, macabre hangman's drop-rides, fake blood and actors dressed up as torturers and gory criminals (including Jack the Ripper and Sweeney Todd), with interactive scares galore. (www. thedungeons.com/london; County Hall, Westminster Bridge Rd, SE1; adult/child £30/24; ⏱10am-4pm Mon-Wed & Fri, 11am-4pm Thu, 10am-6pm Sat,

Tate-to-Tate Boat

For the most scenic of culture trips, take the **Tate Boat** (one-way adult/child £8.30/4.15) between the Bankside Pier at Tate Modern and the Millbank Pier at its sister museum, Tate Britain (p56).

10am-5pm Sun; 👪; 🚇Waterloo, Westminster)

Southbank Centre

ARTS CENTRE

7 ⊙ MAP P134, B3

The flagship venue of the Southbank Centre, Europe's largest centre for performing and visual arts, is the **Royal Festival Hall**. Its gently curved facade of glass and Portland stone is more humane than its 1970s brutalist neighbours. It is one of London's leading music venues and the epicentre of life on this part of the South Bank, hosting cafes, restaurants, shops and bars. (📞020-3879 9555; www.southbankcentre.co.uk; Belvedere Rd, SE1; 👪; 🚇Waterloo, Embankment)

Old Operating Theatre Museum & Herb Garret

MUSEUM

8 ⊙ MAP P134, G3

This unique museum, 32 steps up a spiral stairway in the tower of **St Thomas Church** (1703), is the unlikely home of Britain's oldest operating theatre. Rediscovered in 1956, the garret was used by the apothecary of St Thomas's Hospital to store medicinal herbs. The museum looks back at the horror of 19th-century medicine – all pre-anaesthetic and pre-antiseptic. You can browse the natural remedies, including snail water for venereal disease, and recoil at the fiendish array of amputation knives and blades. (www.oldoperatingtheatre.com; 9a St Thomas St, SE1; adult/child £6.50/3.50; ⏰10.30am-5pm; 🚇London Bridge)

HMS Belfast

SHIP

9 ⊙ MAP P134, H3

HMS *Belfast* is a magnet for kids of all ages. This large, light cruiser – launched in 1938 – served in WWII, helping to sink the German battleship *Scharnhorst*, shelling the Normandy coast on D-Day and later participating in the Korean War. Its 6in guns could bombard a target 14 land miles distant. Displays offer a great insight into what life on board was like, in peace times and during military engagements. (www.iwm.org.uk/visits/hms-belfast; Queen's Walk, SE1; adult/child £15.45/7.70; ⏰10am-5pm; 🚇London Bridge)

Millennium Bridge

BRIDGE

10 ⊙ MAP P134, E2

The elegant steel, aluminium and concrete Millennium Bridge staples the south bank of the Thames, in front of Tate Modern, to the north bank, at the steps of Peter's Hill below St Paul's Cathedral. The low-slung frame designed by Sir Norman Foster and Antony Caro looks spectacular, particularly when lit up at night with fibre optics, and the view of St Paul's from the South Bank has become one of London's iconic images. (◉St Paul's, Blackfriars)

Shard   NOTABLE BUILDING

11 ◉ MAP P134, G3

Puncturing the skies above London, the dramatic splinter-like form of the Shard has rapidly become an icon of London. The viewing platforms on floors 69 and 72 are open to the public and the views are, as you'd expect from a 244m vantage point, sweeping, but they come at a hefty price – book online at least a day in advance to make a big saving. (www.theview fromtheshard.com; 32 London Bridge St, SE1; adult/child £31/25; ◷10am-10pm; ◉London Bridge)

Eating

Padella   ITALIAN £

Yet another fantastic addition to the foodie enclave of Borough Market (p136), Padella (see 3 ◉ Map p134, F3) is a small, energetic bistro specialising in handmade pasta dishes, inspired by the owners' extensive culinary adventures in Italy. The portions are small, which means that, joy of joys, you can (and should!) have more than one dish. Outstanding. (www.padella.co; 6 Southwark St, SE1; dishes £4-11.50; ◷noon-3.45pm & 5-10pm Mon-Sat, noon-3.45pm & 5-9pm Sun; ✒; ◉London Bridge)

Padella

Pie & Mash

🍴

Those curious to find out how Londoners ate before everything went chic and ethnic should visit a traditional pie-'n'-mash shop. **M Manze** (Map p134, H5; www.manze.co.uk; 87 Tower Bridge Rd, SE1; mains from £2.95; ⏰11am-2pm Mon, 10.30am-2pm Tue-Thu, 10am-2.30pm Fri, to 2.45pm Sat; ⊖Borough) dates to 1902 and is a classic operation, from the ageing tile work to the traditional worker's menu (with prices from £2.95): pie and mash or pie and liquor. You can take your eels jellied or stewed.

Watch House
CAFE £

12 ❌ MAP P134, H5

Saying that the Watch House nails the sandwich wouldn't really do justice to this tip-top cafe: the sandwiches really are delicious, and use artisan breads from a local baker. But there is also great coffee, and treats for the sweet-toothed. The small but lovely setting is a renovated 19th-century watch-house from where guards looked out for grave robbers in the next-door cemetery. (www. thewatchhouse.com; 199 Bermondsey St, SE1; mains from £4.95; ⏰7am-6pm Mon-Fri, 8am-6pm Sat, 9am-5pm Sun; 🖊; ⊖Borough, London Bridge)

Maltby Street Market
MARKET £

13 ❌ MAP P134, H4

Started as an alternative to the juggernaut that is Borough Market (p136), Maltby Street Market is becoming a victim of its own success, with brick-and-mortar shops and restaurants replacing the old workshops, and throngs of visitors. That said, it boasts some original – and all top-notch – food stalls selling smoked salmon from East London, African burgers, seafood and lots of pastries. (www. maltby.st; Maltby St, SE1; dishes £5-10; ⏰9am-4pm Sat, 11am-4pm Sun; ⊖Bermondsey)

Skylon
MODERN EUROPEAN ££

This excellent restaurant (see 24 ⭐ Map p134, B3) inside the Royal Festival Hall (p144) is divided into grill and fine-dining sections by a large bar. The decor is cutting-edge 1950s: muted colours and period chairs (trendy then, trendier now), while floor-to-ceiling windows bathe you in magnificent views of the Thames and the city. Booking is advised. (📞020-7654 7800; www.skylon-restaurant.co.uk; 3rd fl, Royal Festival Hall, Southbank Centre, Belvedere Rd, SE1; 3-course menu grill/restaurant £25/30; ⏰grill noon-11pm Mon-Sat, to 10.30pm Sun, restaurant noon-2.30pm & 5-10.30pm Mon-Sat, 11.30am-4pm Sun; 📶; ⊖Waterloo)

Anchor & Hope

GASTROPUB ££

14 ⊗ MAP P134, C4

A stalwart of the South Bank food scene, the Anchor & Hope is a quintessential gastropub: elegant but not formal, and utterly delicious (European fare with a British twist). The menu changes daily but think salt-marsh lamb shoulder cooked for seven hours; wild rabbit with anchovies, almonds and rocket; and panna cotta with rhubarb compote. (www.anchorandhopepub.co.uk; 36 The Cut, SE1; mains £12-20; ⊙noon-2.30pm Tue-Sat, 6-10.30pm Mon-Sat, 12.30-3.15pm Sun; ⊖Southwark)

Baltic

EASTERN EUROPEAN ££

15 ⊗ MAP P134, D4

In a bright and airy, high-ceilinged dining room with glass roof and wooden beams, Baltic is travel on a plate: dill and beetroot, dumplings and blini, pickle and smoke, rich stews and braised meat. From Polish to Georgian, the flavours are authentic and the dishes beautifully presented. The wine and vodka lists are equally diverse. (☎020-7928 1111; www.balticrestaurant.co.uk; 74 Blackfriars Rd, SE1; mains £11.50-22, 2-course lunch menu £17.50; ⊙noon-3pm & 5.30-11.15pm Tue-Sat, noon-4.30pm & 5.30-10.30pm Sun, 5.30-11.15pm Mon; 🎤; ⊖Southwark)

Tate Modern & South Bank Eating

Shakespeare's Globe (p136)

PB&S PANAYOTOV/SHUTTERSTOCK ©

Arabica Bar & Kitchen

MIDDLE EASTERN £££

16 🍴 MAP P134, F3

Pan–Middle Eastern cuisine is a well-rehearsed classic these days, but Arabica Bar & Kitchen has managed to bring something fresh to its table: the decor is contemporary and bright, the food delicate and light, and there's an emphasis on sharing (two to three small dishes per person). The downside of this tapas approach is that the bill adds up quickly. (📞 020-3011 5151; www.arabicabarandkitchen.com; 3 Rochester Walk, Borough Market, SE1; dishes £6-14; 🕐 noon-11pm Mon-Fri, 9am-11.30pm Sat, noon-9pm Sun; 🚀; 🚇 London Bridge)

Drinking

Oblix

BAR

On the 32nd floor of the Shard (p139), Oblix (see 11 🔘 MAP p134, G3) offers mesmerising vistas of London. You can come for anything from a coffee (£3.50) to a cocktail (from £13.50) and enjoy virtually the same views as the official viewing galleries of the Shard (but at a reduced cost and with the added bonus of a drink). Live music every night from 7pm. (www.oblixrestaurant. com; 32nd fl, Shard, 31 St Thomas St, SE1; 🕐 noon-11pm; 🚇 London Bridge)

King's Arms

PUB

17 🍺 MAP P134, C3

Relaxed and charming, this neighbourhood boozer at the corner of a terraced Waterloo backstreet

was a funeral parlour in a previous life. The large traditional bar area, complete with open fire in winter, serves up a good selection of ales and bitters. It gets packed with after-work crowds between 6pm and 8pm. (📞 020-7207 0784; www.thekingsarmslondon.co.uk; 25 Roupell St, SE1; 🕐 11am-11pm Mon-Fri, noon-11pm Sat, noon-10.30pm Sun; 🚇 Waterloo)

Coffee House

COFFEE

18 ☕ MAP P134, F4

This addition to the Bankside coffee scene is a godsend, and for barista-worshipping coffee lovers it's the place to come. There may be a slight whiff of pretension about the Mac-wielding media types who choose to hang out here, but it's still a top spot with enough space to linger peacefully over a flat white. (The Gentlemen Baristas; www.thegentlemenbaristas.com; 63 Union St, SE1; coffee £1.50-2.90; 🕐 7am-6pm Mon-Fri, 8.30am-5pm Sat, 10am-4pm Sun; 🛜; 🚇 London Bridge, Borough)

George Inn

PUB

19 🍺 MAP P134, F3

Owned and leased by the National Trust, this magnificent old boozer is London's last surviving galleried coaching inn, dating from 1677 (after a fire destroyed it the year before) and mentioned in Dickens' *Little Dorrit*. It is on the site of the Tabard Inn, where the pilgrims in Chaucer's *The Canterbury Tales* gathered before setting out on the road to Canterbury, Kent. (NT;

Bermondsey Beer Mile

Craft beer is having its moment in London, and Bermondsey is at the epicentre of this revival, with seven microbreweries within just over a mile, welcoming discerning drinkers on Friday nights and Saturdays generally from 11am to 5pm (sometimes later).

Try **Southwark Brewing Company** (www.southwarkbrewing.co.uk; 46 Druid St, SE1; ⏱5-10pm Fri, 11am-6pm Sat, to 4pm Sun; ⊖London Bridge), located in a hangar-like space kitted out with big tables and sofas. Also worthy is **Anspach & Hobday** (www.anspachandhobday. com; 118 Druid St, SE1; ⏱5-9.30pm Fri, 10.30am-6.30pm Sat, 12.30-5pm Sun; ⊖London Bridge), which has a nice outdoor seating area. Porter (a dark, roasted beer) is the name of the game here.

📞020-7407 2056; www.nationaltrust.org.uk/george-inn; 77 Borough High St, SE1; ⏱11am-11pm; ⊖London Bridge)

Aqua Shard — BAR

Entry to this classy three-storey bar and restaurant (see 11 ◉ Map p134, G3) gets you the mesmeric view from the Shard (p139), without the sky-high viewing-platform admission fee. There are often queues, and the bar doesn't take bookings (though the restaurant does), so come early (for coffee) or very late (close to midnight) if you want to avoid a wait. Children are welcome until 6pm. (www.aquashard.co.uk; 31st fl, 31 St Thomas St, SE1; ⏱10.30am-1am Sun-Thu, to 3am Fri & Sat; ⊖London Bridge)

Anchor Bankside — PUB

20 🍺 MAP P134, F3

A mainstay recommendation – but with good reason – this riverside boozer dates back to the 17th century. Trips to the terrace are rewarded with superb views across the Thames but brace for a constant deluge of drinkers. Eighteenth-century dictionary writer Samuel Johnson, whose brewer friend owned the joint, drank here, as did diarist Samuel Pepys before that. (34 Park St, SE1; ⏱11am-11pm Sun-Wed, to midnight Thu-Sat; ⊖London Bridge)

Entertainment

Shakespeare's Globe — THEATRE

If you love Shakespeare and the theatre, the Globe (see 2 ◉ Map p134, E2) will knock your theatrical socks off. This authentic Shakespearean theatre (p136) is a wooden 'O' without a roof over the central stage area, and although there are covered wooden bench seats in tiers around the stage, many people (there's room for 700) do as 17th-century 'groundlings' did, and stand in front of the stage. (📞020-7401 9919; www.

shakespearesglobe.com; 21 New Globe Walk, SE1; seats £20-45, standing £5; ⊖Blackfriars, London Bridge)

National Theatre   THEATRE

21 ⭐ MAP P134, B3

England's flagship theatre showcases a mix of classic and contemporary plays performed by excellent casts in three theatres (Olivier, Lyttelton and Dorfman). Artistic director Rufus Norris, who started in April 2015, made headlines in 2016 for announcing plans to stage a Brexit-based drama. (Royal National Theatre; ☎020-7452 3000; www.nationaltheatre.org.uk; South Bank, SE1; ⊖Waterloo)

Unicorn Theatre   THEATRE

22 ⭐ MAP P134, H3

It seems only natural that one of the first theatres dedicated to young audiences would make its home in a neighbourhood of heavy-hitting theatres. Its rationale is that the best theatre for children should be judged against the same standards as the best theatre for adults. The productions are therefore excellent, wide-ranging and perfectly tailored to their target audience. (☎020-7645 0560; www.unicorntheatre.com; 147 Tooley St, SE1; ⊖London Bridge)

Old Vic   THEATRE

23 ⭐ MAP P134, C4

American actor Kevin Spacey took the theatrical helm of this London theatre in 2003. He was suc-

ceeded in April 2015 by Matthew Warchus (who directed *Matilda the Musical* and the film *Pride*), whose aim is to bring eclectic programming to the theatre: expect new writing, as well as dynamic revivals of old works and musicals. (☎0844 871 7628; www.oldvictheatre.com; The Cut, SE1; ⊖Waterloo)

Southbank Centre   CONCERT VENUE

The Southbank Centre (see 7 ◉ Map p134, B3) comprises several venues – Royal Festival Hall, Queen Elizabeth Hall and Purcell Room – hosting a wide range of performing arts. As well as regular programming, it organises fantastic festivals, including **London Wonderground** (circus and cabaret), **Udderbelly** (a festival of comedy in all its guises) and **Meltdown** (a music event curated by the best and most eclectic names in music). (☎0844 875 0073; www.southbankcentre.co.uk; Belvedere Rd, SE1; ⊖Waterloo)

Royal Festival Hall   CONCERT VENUE

24 ⭐ MAP P134, B3

Royal Festival Hall's amphitheatre seats 2500 and is one of the best places for catching world- and classical-music artists. The sound is fantastic, the programming impeccable and there are frequent free gigs in the wonderfully expansive foyer. (☎020-7960 4200; www.southbankcentre.co.uk; Southbank Centre, Belvedere Rd, SE1; 📶; ⊖Waterloo)

Queen Elizabeth Hall
CONCERT VENUE

25 ⭐ MAP P134, B3

This concert hall hosts music and dance performances on a smaller scale to the nearby Royal Festival Hall, both part of the Southbank Centre. The Hall reopened in April 2018 after its 21st-century facelift. (QEH; www.southbankcentre.co.uk; Southbank Centre, Belvedere Rd, SE1; ⊖Waterloo)

Rambert Dance Company
DANCE

26 ⭐ MAP P134, B3

The innovative Rambert Dance Company is the UK's foremost contemporary dance troupe, performing at venues across London, the UK and abroad. (☑020-8630 0600; www.rambert.org.uk; 99 Upper Ground, SE1)

Shopping

Lovely & British
GIFTS & SOUVENIRS

27 🔒 MAP P134, H4

As the name suggests, this gorgeous Bermondsey bou-

tique prides itself on stocking prints, jewellery and homewares (crockery especially) from British designers. It's an eclectic mix of wares, with very reasonable prices, which make lovely presents or souvenirs. (☑020-7378 6570; www.facebook.com/LovelyandBritish; 132a Bermondsey St, SE1; ⊘10am-6pm Mon-Fri, to 7pm Sat, 11am-5pm Sun; ⊖London Bridge)

Utobeer
FOOD & DRINKS

This beer shop (see 3 ◉ Map p134, F3) inside Borough Market (p136) stocks around 700 international bottled beers, with a large selection of both American and European brews to take away. Its sister pub, The Rake, (p63) is located just outside the market. (www.utobeer.co.uk; Borough Market, Unit 24, Middle Row, SE1; ⊘11am-5.30pm Mon-Fri, 9am-5pm Sat; ⊖London Bridge)

Explore ◈

Kensington Museums

Splendidly well groomed, Kensington is one of London's most handsome neighbourhoods. You'll find three fine museums here – the V&A, the Natural History Museum and the Science Museum – as well as excellent dining and shopping, graceful parklands and elegant streets of grand period architecture.

Make a start with the bountiful Victoria & Albert Museum (p148), bearing in mind that you could easily spend the entire day – or more – in this one museum alone. If you have children, aim instead for the Natural History Museum (p152) or the Science Museum (p158), both enthralling for young ones and tots. For lunch, dine at the V&A Café (p149). Burn off your lunch by exploring central London's glorious green expanses: Hyde Park (p158) and Kensington Gardens (p160) will delight adults and children with their galleries, play areas and Kensington Palace (p158). If you're in London to shop, you're in the right place: walk the length and breadth of Old Brompton Rd, with a compulsory stop at Harrods (p165) but don't overlook Kensington High Street and the King's Rd.

Getting There & Around

⊖ Hyde Park Corner, Knightsbridge and South Kensington (Piccadilly Line) and South Kensington, Sloane Sq and High St Kensington (Circle & District Lines).

🚌 Handy routes include 74, 52 and 360.

Kensington Map on p156

Serpentine Lake, Hyde Park (p158) | WEI HUANG/SHUTTERSTOCK ©

Top Sight 📷
Victoria & Albert Museum

Specialising in decorative art and design, the museum universally known as the V&A hosts some 2.75 million objects from Britain and around the globe, reaching back as far as 5000 years. This unparalleled collection is displayed in a setting as inspiring as the sheer diversity and (often exquisite) rarity of its exhibits.

◎ MAP P156, E5

📞 020-7942 2000

www.vam.ac.uk

Cromwell Rd, SW7

admission free

🕐 10am-5.45pm Sat-Thu, to 10pm Fri

Ⓣ South Kensington

Collection

Through 146 galleries, the museum houses the world's greatest collection of decorative arts, from ancient Chinese ceramics to modernist architectural drawings, Korean bronze and Japanese swords, cartoons by Raphael, gowns from the Elizabethan era, ancient jewellery, a Sony Walkman – and much, much more. The museum is open till 10pm on Friday evenings, although the number of open galleries is reduced.

Entrance

Entering under the stunning blue-and-yellow blown-glass **chandelier** by Dale Chihuly, you can grab a museum map (£1 donation requested) at the information desk. (If the 'Grand Entrance' on Cromwell Rd is too busy, there's another around the corner on Exhibition Rd, or you can enter from the tunnel in the basement, if arriving by tube.) A new entrance on Exhibition Rd was unveiled in 2017.

Level 1

The street level is mostly devoted to art and design from India, China, Japan, Korea and Southeast Asia, as well as European art. One of the museum's highlights is the **Cast Courts** in rooms 46a and 46b, containing staggering plaster casts collected in the Victorian era, such as Michelangelo's David, acquired in 1858.

The **TT Tsui (China) Gallery** (rooms 44 and 47e) displays lovely pieces, including a beautifully lithe wooden statue of Guanyin (a Mahayana bodhisattva) seated in a regal *lalitasana* pose from AD 1200; also check out a leaf from the 'Twenty Views of the Yuanmingyuan Summer Palace' (1781–86), revealing the Haiyantang and the 12 animal heads of the fountain (now ruins) in Beijing. Within the subdued lighting of the **Japan Gallery** (room 45) stands a fearsome **suit of armour** in the Domaru style. More than

★ Top Tips

o Visit late nights on Fridays, when there are fewer visitors.

o Work out what you want to see and how to reach it before you visit.

o Grab one of the maps (£1) from the information desk.

✕ Take a Break

Perfect for a breather, the **V&A Cafe** (📞 020-7581 2159; mains £7.45-13.50; ⏰10am-5.15pm Sat-Thu, to 9.30pm Fri; 📶) is a picture; the afternoon tea is a choice occasion.

For scrummy Lebanese cuisine, leg it to Comptoir Libanais (p162) round the corner from South Kensington tube station.

400 objects are within the **Islamic Middle East Gallery** (room 42), including ceramics, textiles, carpets, glass and woodwork from the 8th century up to the years before WWI. The exhibition's highlight is the gorgeous mid-16th-century **Ardabil Carpet**.

John Madejski Garden & Refreshment Rooms

For fresh air, the landscaped John Madejski Garden is a lovely shaded inner courtyard. Cross it to reach the original Refreshment Rooms (Morris, Gamble and Poynter Rooms), dating from the 1860s and redesigned by McInnes Usher McKnight Architects (MUMA), who also renovated the **Medieval and Renaissance galleries** (1350–1600) to the right of the Grand Entrance.

Level 2 & 4

The **British Galleries**, featuring every aspect of British design from 1500 to 1900, are divided between levels 2 (1500–1760) and 4 (1760–1900). Level 4 also boasts the **Architecture Gallery** (rooms 127 to 128a), which vividly describes architectural styles via models and videos, and the spectacular, brightly illuminated **Contemporary Glass Gallery** (room 129).

Level 3

The **Jewellery Gallery** (rooms 91 to 93) is outstanding; the mezzanine level – accessed via the glass-and-perspex spiral staircase – glitters with jewel-encrusted swords, watches and gold boxes. The **Photographs Gallery** (room 100) is one of the nation's best, with access to over 500,000 images collected since the mid-19th century. **Design Since 1945** (room 76) celebrates design classics from a 1985 Sony credit-card radio to a 1992 Nike 'Air Max' shoe, Peter Ghyczy's Garden Egg Chair from 1968 and the now ubiquitous selfie stick.

Level 6

Among the pieces in the **Ceramics Gallery** (rooms 136 to 146) – the world's largest – are standout items from the Middle East and Asia. The **Dr Susan Weber Gallery** (rooms 133 to 135) celebrates furniture design over the past six centuries.

Temporary Exhibitions

The V&A's temporary exhibitions – covering anything from David Bowie retrospectives to designer Alexander McQueen, special materials and trends – are compelling and fun (admission fees apply). There are also talks, workshops, events and one of the best museum shops around.

V&A Tours

Free one-hour guided introductory tours leave the main reception area every day at 10.30am, 12.30pm, 1.30pm and 3.30pm. Check the website for details of other, more specific, tours.

V&A Through the Ages

The V&A opened in 1852 on the back of the runaway success of the Great Exhibition of 1851 and Prince Albert's enthusiasm for the arts. Its aims were to make art available to all, and to effect 'improvement of public taste in design'. It began with objects first collected by the Government School of Design in the 1830s and '40s and £5000 worth of purchases from the Great Exhibition profits.

Early Expansion

The Museum of Manufactures, as it was then known, moved its eclectic mix of designs and innovations to a collection of semi-permanent buildings in South Kensington in 1857. An expansion brought more ad hoc structures, and in 1890 the museum's board launched a competition to design the museum's new facade on Cromwell Rd and bring harmony to its architectural hotchpotch. Young architect Aston Webb (who went on to design the facade of Buckingham Palace) won, and Queen Victoria laid the foundation stone in May 1899. The occasion marked a name change, becoming the Victoria & Albert Museum.

Scrapping Admission Charges

When militant suffragettes threatened to damage exhibits at public museums in 1913, the V&A considered denying women entry to the museum, but instead opted for scrapping admission charges to the museum to boost visitor numbers and so help protect the V&A's collection.

V&A in the Wars

The V&A remained open during both world wars. When WWI broke out, several of French sculptor Auguste Rodin's works were on loan at the V&A and the hostilities prevented their return to France. Rodin was so moved by the solidarity of English and French troops that he donated the pieces to the museum. During WWII the museum was hit repeatedly by German bombs (a commemorative inscription remains on Cromwell Rd). Much of the collection had been evacuated (or, as with Raphael's cartoons, bricked in), so damage was minimal.

The Exhibition Road Building Project

The Exhibition Road Building Project opened a magnificent new entrance – via the 19th-century screen designed by Sir Aston Webb – leading to the new Sackler Courtyard, as well as the subterranean Sainsbury Gallery, a vast new venue for temporary exhibitions.

Top Sight 📷
Natural History Museum

One of London's best-loved museums, this colossal landmark is infused with the irrepressible Victorian spirit of collecting, cataloguing and interpreting the natural world. The main museum building, designed by Alfred Waterhouse in blue and sand-coloured brick and terracotta, is as much a reason to visit as the world-famous collection within. Kids are the number-one fans, but adults are as enamoured of the exhibits as their inquisitive offspring.

◉ MAP P156, D5

www.nhm.ac.uk
Cromwell Rd, SW7
admission free
🕙 10am-5.50pm
🚇 South Kensington

Architecture

Be sure to admire the astonishing architecture of Alfred Waterhouse. With carved pillars, animal bas-reliefs, sculptures of plants and beasts, leaded windows and sublime arches, the museum is a work of art and a labour of love.

Hintze Hall

This grand central hall resembles a cathedral nave – quite fitting, as it was built in a time when the natural sciences were challenging the biblical tenets of Christian orthodoxy. Naturalist and first superintendent of the museum Richard Owen celebrated the building as a 'cathedral to nature'.

After 81 years in the Mammals Hall, in 2017 the blue whale skeleton was relocated to Hintze Hall, with the famous cast of a **diplodocus skeleton** (nicknamed Dippy) making way for the colossal mammal. The transfer itself was a mammoth and painstaking engineering project, disassembling and preparing the 4.5-tonne bones for reconstruction in a dramatic diving posture that will greet visitors to the museum.

Green Zone

While children love the Blue Zone, adults may prefer the Green Zone, especially the **Treasures in Cadogan Gallery**, on the 1st floor, which houses the museum's most prized possessions, each with a unique history. Exhibits include a chunk of moon rock, an Emperor Penguin egg collected by Captain Scott's expedition and a first edition of Charles Darwin's *On the Origin of Species*.

Equally rare and exceptional are the gems and rocks held in the **Vault**, including a Martian meteorite and the largest emerald ever found.

Take a moment to marvel at the trunk section of a 1300-year-old **giant sequoia tree** on the 2nd floor: its size is mind-boggling.

★ Top Tips

○ Hop on an after-hours museum tour for a unique perspective in an almost empty museum.

○ More than five million visitors come annually – avoid school holidays and weekends; otherwise, get here early.

○ Ticket holders to ticketed exhibitions get priority access, to beat the queues.

○ Download the visitor app for details of the top draws and exhibitions.

✗ Take a Break

For a pint in a classic and gloriously inviting London mews setting, head to the nearby **Queen's Arms** (www.thequeensarmskensington.co.uk; 30 Queen's Gate Mews, SW7; ☺ noon-11pm Mon-Sat, to 10.30pm Sun).

Polish restaurant **Daquise** (www.daquise.co.uk; 20 Thurloe St, SW7; mains £15-20; ☺ noon-11pm) near South Kensington tube station cooks up a fine express lunch.

Back on the ground floor, the **Creepy Crawlies Gallery** is fantastic, delving into every aspect of insect life and whether they are our friends or foes (both!).

Blue Zone

Undoubtedly the museum's star attraction, the **Dinosaurs Gallery** takes you on an impressive overhead walkway, past a dromaeosaurus (a small and agile meat eater) before reaching a roaring animatronic T rex and then winding its way through skeletons, fossils, casts and fascinating displays about how dinosaurs lived and died.

Another highlight of this zone is the **Mammals & Blue Whale Gallery**, with its life-size blue whale model and extensive displays on cetaceans.

Lest we forget we are part of the animal kingdom, the museum has also dedicated a gallery to **Human Biology**, where you'll be able to understand more about what makes us tick (senses, hormones, our brain and so on).

Red Zone

This zone explores the ever-changing nature of our planet and the forces shaping it. The earthquake simulator (in the **Volcanoes and Earthquakes Gallery**), which recreates the 1995 Kobe earthquake in a grocery store (of which you can see footage) is a favourite, as is the **From the Beginning Gallery**, which retraces Earth's history.

In **Earth's Treasury**, you can find out more about our planet's mineral riches and how they are being used in

our everyday lives – from jewellery to construction and electronics.

Access to most of the galleries in the Red Zone is via **Earth Hall** and a very tall escalator that disappears into a huge metal sculpture of the Earth. The most intact **stegosaurus fossil skeleton** ever found is displayed at the base.

Orange Zone

The **Darwin Centre** is the beating heart of the museum: this is where the museum's millions of specimens are kept and where its scientists work. The top two floors of the amazing 'cocoon' building are dedicated to explaining the kind of research the museum does (and how) – windows allow you to see the researchers at work.

If you'd like to find out more, pop into the **Attenborough studio** (named after famous naturalist and broadcaster David Attenborough) for one of the daily talks with the museum's scientists. The studio also shows films throughout the day.

Wildlife Garden

Due to be hugely expanded, this slice of English countryside in SW7 encompasses a range of British lowland habitats, including a meadow with farm gates, a bee tree where a colony of honey bees fills the air, and a pond. Late summer sees the arrival of Grey face Dartmoor sheep. Ornithologists

Exhibitions

The museum hosts regular exhibitions (admission fees apply), some of them on a recurrent basis. **Wildlife Photographer of the Year** (Sep-Oct; adult/child £13.50/8, family £28-38), with its show-stopping images, is now in its 50th year, and **Sensational Butterflies** (Apr-Sep; per person £5.85, family £19.80), a tunnel tent on the East Lawn that swarms with what must originally have been called 'flutter-bys', has become a firm summer favourite.

can look out for moorhens, wrens and finches.

Museum Shop

As well as the obligatory dinosaur figurines and animal soft toys, the museum's shop has a huge and brilliant collection of children's books about nature, animals and, of course, dinosaurs. On the adult side, beautiful jewellery and lovely stationery are treats to look out for.

Ice Skating at the Museum

From Halloween to January, a section by the East Lawn of the museum is transformed into a glittering and highly popular ice rink, complete with a hot-drinks stall. Our advice: book your slot well ahead, browse the museum and skate later.

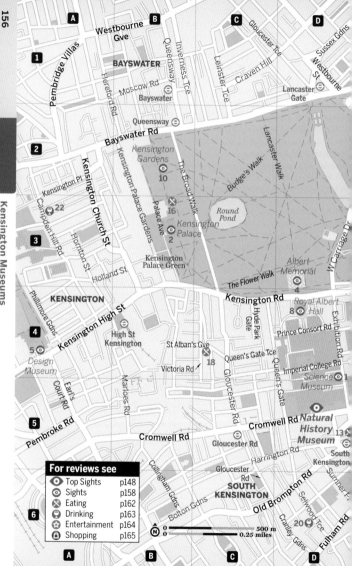

Kensington Museums

A **B** **C** **D**

1 Pembridge Villas · Westbourne Gve · Queensway · Inverness Tce · Gloucester Tce · Craven Hill · Leinster Tce · Sussex Gdns · Westbourne St

BAYSWATER

Moscow Rd
Bayswater
Hereford Rd

2 Queensway ⊜

Bayswater Rd

Lancaster Gate ⊜

Lancaster Walk

Kensington Gardens
10 ⊙

Kensington Church St
Kensington Pl
Campden Hill Rd
22 ⊙

3 Horton St
Holland St

The Broad Walk
Palace Ave
16 ⊗
Kensington Palace
2 ⊙

Budge's Walk

Round Pond

W Carriage Dr

Kensington Palace Gardens
Kensington Palace Green

Albert Memorial
4 ⊙

The Flower Walk

Kensington Rd

Royal Albert Hall
8 ⊙

KENSINGTON
Phillimore Gdns

4 Kensington High St
High St Kensington ⊜
St Alban's Gve ⊗
18
Victoria Rd

Hyde Park Gate
Queen's Gate Tce
Prince Consort Rd
Queen's Gate
Exhibition Rd

Imperial College Rd
Science Museum ⊙ 1

5 ⊙
Design Museum
Earl's Court Rd

Marloes Rd

Gloucester Rd

Natural History Museum ⊙ 13

5 Pembroke Rd
Cromwell Rd
Gloucester Rd

Cromwell Rd

South Kensington ⊜

Harrington Rd
Collingham Gdns
Gloucester Rd
SOUTH KENSINGTON
Bolton Gdns

Sumner Pl
Old Brompton Rd
Selwood Tce
20 ⊙
Cranley Gdns
Fulham Rd

For reviews see
⊙ Top Sights p148
⊙ Sights p158
⊗ Eating p162
☕ Drinking p163
☆ Entertainment p164
🔒 Shopping p165

6

N
0 ——————— 500 m
0 ——————— 0.25 miles

A **B** **C** **D**

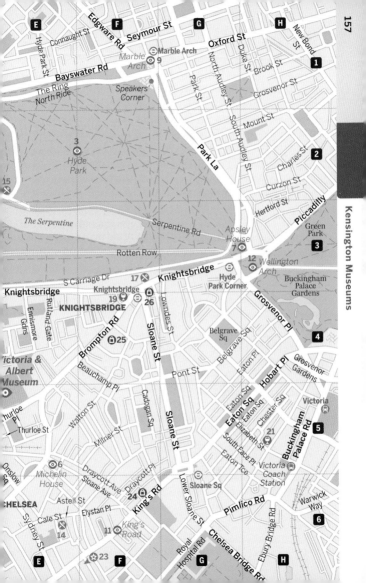

E
Hyde Park Corner
Connaught St

F
Edgware Rd
Seymour St

G
Oxford St
Duke St

H
New Bond St

Bayswater Rd

Marble Arch
9
North Audley St
Brook St

Grosvenor St

1

The Ring
North Ride
Speakers'
Corner

Park St
South Audley St
Mount St

3
Hyde
Park

Park La

Charles St

Curzon St

2

Hertford St

Piccadilly

15

The Serpentine
Serpentine Rd

Apsley
House
7

12
Wellington
Arch

Green
Park

3

Rotten Row

S Carriage Dr
17

Knightsbridge

Knightsbridge
19

Hyde
Park
Corner

Buckingham
Palace
Gardens

Knightsbridge

KNIGHTSBRIDGE
26

Lowndes St

Grosvenor Pl

4

Ennismore
Gdns
Rutland Gate

Brompton Rd
25

Sloane St

Belgrave
Sq

Belgrave Pl

Eaton Pl

Hobart Pl

Grosvenor
Gardens

Victoria &
Albert
Museum

Beauchamp Pl

Pont St

Cadogan Sq

Walton St

Eaton Sq
Eaton Sq
Eaton Sq

Chester Sq

Victoria

5

Thurloe
Pl

Thurloe St

Milner St

Sloane St

Elizabeth St

21

Buckingham Palace Rd

Onslow
Sq

6
Michelin
House

Draycott Ave
Sloane Ave
Draycott Pl
24

South Eaton Pl

Eaton Tce

Victoria
Coach
Station

CHELSEA

Astell St
Cale St
Elystan Pl
14

King's Rd

Lower Sloane St

Sloane Sq

Pimlico Rd

Warwick
Way

6

Sydney St

11
King's
Road
23

Royal Hospital Rd

Chelsea Bridge Rd

Ebury Bridge Rd

E   **F**   **G**   **H**

Sights

Science Museum
MUSEUM

1 MAP P156, D4

With seven floors of interactive
and educational exhibits, this
scientifically spellbinding museum
will mesmerise adults and children
alike, covering everything from
early technology to space travel.
A perennial favourite is **Exploring Space**, a gallery featuring
genuine rockets and satellites and
a full-size replica of the 'Eagle', the
lander that took Neil Armstrong
and Buzz Aldrin to the moon in
1969. The **Making the Modern
World Gallery** next door is a visual
feast of locomotives, planes, cars
and other revolutionary inventions. (020-7942 4000; www.
sciencemuseum.org.uk; Exhibition Rd,
SW7; admission free; 10am-6pm;
South Kensington)

Kensington Palace
PALACE

2 MAP P156, B3

Built in 1605, the palace became
the favourite royal residence
under William and Mary of
Orange in 1689, and remained so
until George III became king and
moved out. Today, it is still a royal
residence, with the likes of the
Duke and Duchess of Cambridge
(Prince William and his wife
Catherine) and Prince Harry living
there. A large part of the palace
is open to the public, however,
including the King's and Queen's
State Apartments. (www.hrp.org.

uk/kensington-palace; Kensington
Gardens, W8; adult/child £15.50/free
(when booked online); 10am-4pm
Nov-Feb, to 6pm Mar-Oct; High St
Kensington)

Hyde Park
PARK

3 MAP P156, F2

At 145 hectares, Hyde Park is central London's largest open space,
expropriated from the Church in
1536 by Henry VIII and turned into
a hunting ground and later a venue
for duels, executions and horse
racing. The 1851 Great Exhibition
was held here, and during WWII
the park became an enormous
potato field. These days, there's
boating on the **Serpentine**, summer concerts (Bruce Springsteen, Florence + The Machine,
Patti Smith), film nights and
other warm-weather events. (www.
royalparks.org.uk/parks/hyde-park;
5am-midnight; Marble Arch, Hyde
Park Corner, Queensway)

Albert Memorial
MONUMENT

4 MAP P156, D3

This splendid Victorian confection
on the southern edge of Kensington Gardens is as ostentatious as
its subject. Purportedly humble,
Queen Victoria's German husband
Albert (1819–61) explicitly insisted
he did not want a monument.
Ignoring the good prince's wishes,
the Lord Mayor instructed George
Gilbert Scott to build the 53m-
high, gaudy Gothic memorial – the
4.25m-tall gilded statue of the
prince, surrounded by 187 figures

Queen's Life Guard 🔭

Catch the Queen's Life Guard (Household Cavalry) departing for Horse Guards Parade at 10.28am (9.28am Sundays) from Hyde Park Barracks for the daily Changing of the Guard, performing a ritual that dates to 1660. They troop via Hyde Park Corner, Constitution Hill and the Mall. It's not as busy as the Changing of the Guard at Buckingham Palace and you can get closer to the action.

representing the continents (Asia, Europe, Africa and America), the arts, industry and science, went up in 1876. (📞 tours 020-8969 0104; Kensington Gardens; tours adult/concession £9/8; 🕐 tours 2pm & 3pm 1st Sun of month Mar-Dec; 🚇 Knightsbridge, Gloucester Rd)

Design Museum   MUSEUM

5 ◉ MAP P156, A4

Relocated in 2016 from its former Thames location to a stunning new £83m home by Holland Park, this slick museum is dedicated to popularising the importance and influence of design in everyday life. With a revolving program of special exhibitions, it's a crucial pit-stop for anyone with an eye for modern and contemporary aesthetics. Splendidly housed in the refitted former Commonwealth Institute (which opened in 1962), the lavish interior – all smooth oak and marble – is itself a design triumph. (📞 020-7940 8790; www.designmuseum.org; 224-238 Kensington High St, W8; admission free; 🕐 10am-6pm, to 8pm 1st Fri of month; 🚇 High St Kensington)

Michelin House   HISTORIC BUILDING

6 ◉ MAP P156, E5

Built for Michelin between 1905 and 1911 by François Espinasse, and completely restored in 1985, the building blurs the stylish line between art nouveau and art deco. The iconic roly-poly Michelin Man (Bibendum) appears in the exquisite modern stained glass (the originals were removed at the outbreak of WWII and stored in the Michelin factory in Stoke-on-Trent, but subsequently vanished), while the lobby is decorated with tiles showing early-20th-century cars. (81 Fulham Rd, SW3; 🚇 South Kensington)

Apsley House   HISTORIC BUILDING

7 ◉ MAP P156, H3

This stunning house, containing exhibits about the Duke of Wellington, who defeated Napoleon Bonaparte at Waterloo, was once the first building to appear when entering London from the west and was therefore known as 'No 1 London'. Wellington memorabilia, including the duke's death mask, fills the basement **gallery**, while an

Speakers' Corner

Frequented by Karl Marx, Vladimir Lenin, George Orwell and William Morris, **Speakers' Corner** (Map p156; F1; Park Lane; ⊖Marble Arch) in the north eastern corner of Hyde Park is traditionally the spot for oratorical acrobatics and soapbox ranting. If you have something to get off your chest, do so on Sunday, although you'll mainly have fringe dwellers, religious fanatics and hecklers for company.

astonishing collection of china and silver, and paintings by Velasquez, Rubens, Van Dyck, Brueghel, Murillo and Goya awaits in the 1st-floor Waterloo Gallery. (☏020-7499 5676; www.english-heritage.org.uk/visit/places/apsley-house; 149 Piccadilly, Hyde Park Corner, W1; adult/child £9.30/5.60, with Wellington Arch £11.20/6.70; ⏱11am-5pm Wed-Sun Apr-Oct, 10am-4pm Sat & Sun Nov-Mar; ⊖Hyde Park Corner)

Royal Albert Hall   HISTORIC BUILDING

8 ◉ MAP P156, D4

Built in 1871 thanks in part to the proceeds of the 1851 Great Exhibition organised by Prince Albert (Queen Victoria's husband), this huge, domed, red-brick amphitheatre, adorned with a frieze of Minton tiles, is Britain's most famous concert venue and home to the BBC's Promenade Concerts (the Proms) every summer. To find out about the hall's intriguing history and royal connections, and to gaze out from the Gallery, book an informative one-hour front-of-house **grand tour** (☏020-7589 8212; adult/child £14/7; ⏱hourly 9.30am-4.30pm). (☏0845 401

5034, box office 020-7589 8212; www.royalalberthall.com; Kensington Gore, SW7; tours £10.75-16.75; ⊖South Kensington)

Marble Arch   MONUMENT

9 ◉ MAP P156, F1

Designed by John Nash in 1828, this huge white arch was moved here from its original spot in front of Buckingham Palace in 1851, when adjudged too unimposing an entrance to the royal manor. If you're feeling anarchic, walk through the central portal, a privilege reserved by (unenforced) law for the Royal Family and the ceremonial King's Troop Royal Horse Artillery. (⊖Marble Arch)

Kensington Gardens   PARK

10 ◉ MAP P156, B2

A gorgeous collection of manicured lawns, tree-shaded avenues and basins immediately west of Hyde Park, the picturesque 107-hectare expanse of Kensington Gardens is technically part of Kensington Palace, located in the far west of the gardens. The large

Round Pond is enjoyable to amble around and also worth a look are the lovely fountains in the **Italian Gardens** (Kensington Gardens; 🚇Lancaster Gate), believed to be a gift from Albert to Queen Victoria; they are now the venue of a handy new cafe. (📞0300 061 2000; www. royalparks.org.uk/parks/kensington-gardens; 🕐6am-dusk; 🚇Queensway, Lancaster Gate)

King's Road   STREET

11 ◎ MAP P156, F6

At the counter-cultural forefront of London fashion during the technicolour '60s and anarchic '70s (Ian Fleming's fictional spy James Bond had a flat in a square off the road), the King's Rd today is more a stamping ground for the leisure-class shopping set. The last green-haired Mohawk punks – once tourist sights in themselves – shuffled off sometime in the 1990s. Today it's all Bang & Olufsen, Kurt Geiger and a sprinkling of specialist shops; even pet canines are slim and snappily dressed. (🚇Sloane Sq)

Wellington Arch   MUSEUM

12 ◎ MAP P156, H3

Dominating the green space throttled by the Hyde Park Corner roundabout, this imposing neoclassical 1826 arch originally faced the Hyde Park Screen, but was shunted here in 1882 for road widening. Once a police station, it is now a gallery with temporary exhibitions and a permanent display about the history of the arch. The open-air balconies (accessible

Royal Albert Hall

by lift) afford unforgettable views of Hyde Park, Buckingham Palace and the Mall. (www.english-heritage. org.uk/visit/places/wellington-arch; Hyde Park Corner, W1; adult/child £5/3, with Apsley House £11.20/6.70; ⏱10am-6pm Apr-Sep, to 4pm Nov-Mar; ⊖Hyde Park Corner)

Eating

Comptoir Libanais   LEBANESE £

13 🍴 MAP P156, D5

If your battery's flat hoovering up South Kensington's museums, this colourful, good-looking and brisk restaurant just round the corner from the tube station is a moreish stop for Lebanese mezze, wraps, tagine (slow-cooked casseroles), *mana'esh* (flatbreads), salads and fine breakfasts. When the sun's shining, the outside tables quickly fill with munchers and people-watchers. There are no reservations, so just turn up (elbows sharpened). (📞020-7225 5006; www. comptoirlibanais.com; 1-5 Exhibition Rd, SW7; mains from £8.50; ⏱8.30am-midnight Mon-Sat, to 10.30pm Sun; 📶; ⊖South Kensington)

Tom's Kitchen   MODERN EUROPEAN ££

14 🍴 MAP P156, E6

Recipe for success: mix one part relaxed and smiling staff, and one part light and airy decor to two parts divine food and voila: you have Tom's Kitchen. Classics such as grilled steaks, burgers, slow-cooked pork belly and chicken

schnitzel are cooked to perfection, while seasonal choices such as the homemade ricotta or pan-fried scallops are sublime. (📞020-7349 0202; www.tomskitchen.co.uk/chelsea; 27 Cale St, SW3; mains £16-28; ⏱8am-2.30pm & 6-10.30pm Mon-Fri, 9.30am-3.30pm & 6-10.30pm Sat, to 9.30pm Sun; 📶📶; ⊖South Kensington)

Magazine   INTERNATIONAL ££

15 🍴 MAP P156, E2

Located in the elegant extension of the **Serpentine Sackler Gallery** (📞020-7402 6075; www. serpentinegalleries.org; admission free; ⏱10am-6pm Tue-Sun), Magazine is no ordinary museum cafe. The food is as contemporary and elegant as the building, and artworks from current exhibitions add yet another dimension. The afternoon tea (£25, with one cocktail) is particularly original: out with cucumber sandwiches, in with gin-cured sea trout, goat's curd and coconut granita. (📞020-7298 7552; www.magazine-restaurant.co.uk; West Carriage Dr, W2; mains £13-24, 2-/3-course lunch menu £17.50/21.50; ⏱9am-6pm Tue-Sat; 📶; ⊖Lancaster Gate, Knightsbridge)

Orangery   CAFE ££

16 🍴 MAP P156, B3

The Orangery, housed in an 18th-century conservatory on the grounds of Kensington Palace (p158), is lovely for a late breakfast or lunch, but the standout experience here is English afternoon tea. Book ahead to bag a table on the beautiful terrace. (📞020-3166 6113; www.orangerykensingtonpalace.co.uk; Kensington Palace, Kensington Gardens, W8; mains £12.50-16.50, afternoon tea £27.50; 🕐10am-5pm; 🚻; Ⓔ Queensway, High St Kensington)

Dinner by Heston Blumenthal
MODERN BRITISH £££

17 🍴 MAP P156, F3

Sumptuously presented Dinner is a gastronomic tour de force, taking diners on a journey through British culinary history (with inventive modern inflections). Dishes carry historical dates to convey context, while the restaurant interior is a design triumph, from the glass-walled kitchen and its overhead clock mechanism to the large windows looking onto the park. Book ahead. (📞020-7201 3833; www.dinnerbyheston.com; Mandarin Oriental Hyde Park, 66 Knightsbridge, SW1; 3-course set lunch £45, mains £30-49; 🕐noon-2pm & 6-10.15pm Mon-Fri, noon-2.30pm & 6-10.30pm Sat & Sun; 🛜; Ⓔ Knightsbridge)

Launceston Place
MODERN BRITISH £££

18 🍴 MAP P156, C4

This exceptionally handsome, superchic Michelin-starred restaurant is hidden away almost anonymously on a picture-postcard Kensington street of Edwardian houses. Prepared by London chef Ben Murphy, dishes occupy the acme of gastronomic pleasures and are accompanied by an award-winning wine list. The adventurous will aim

for the six-course tasting menu (£75; vegetarian version available) or the 'reduced' five-course version (£49). (📞020-7937 6912; www.launcestonplace-restaurant.co.uk; 1a Launceston Pl, W8; 2-/3-course set lunch £25/30, 3-course dinner £30-60; 🕐noon-2.30pm Wed-Sat, to 3.30pm Sun, 6-10pm Tue-Sat, 6.30-9pm Sun; 🛜; Ⓔ Gloucester Rd, High St Kensington)

Drinking

Buddha Bar
BAR

19 🍺 MAP P156, F4

When you've shopped your legs off in Knightsbridge, this serenely seductive zone welcomes you into a world of Chinese bird-cage lanterns, subdued lighting, tucked-away corners and booths, perfect for sipping on a Singapore Sling and chilling out. The restaurant downstairs continues the Oriental theme, serving pan-Asian specialities. (📞020-3667 5222; www.buddhabarlondon.com; 145 Knightsbridge, SW1; cocktails from £15; 🕐5pm-midnight Mon-Fri, noon-midnight Sat, to 11.30pm Sun; 🛜; Ⓔ Knightsbridge)

Anglesea Arms
PUB

20 🍺 MAP P156, D6

Seasoned with age and decades of ale-quaffing patrons (including Charles Dickens, who lived on the same road, and DH Lawrence), this old-school pub boasts considerable character and a strong showing of brews, while the terrace out front swarms with punters in warmer months. Arch-criminal Bruce Reynolds master-minded the Great Train Robbery over drinks here. (020-7373 7960; www.angleseaarms.com; 15 Selwood Tce, SW7; 11am-11pm Mon-Sat, noon-10.30pm Sun; South Kensington)

Tomtom Coffee House CAFE

21 MAP P156, H5

Tomtom has built its reputation on its amazing coffee: not only are the drinks fabulously presented (forget ferns and hearts in your latte, here it's peacocks fanning their tails), but the selection is dizzying; from the usual espresso-based suspects to filter, and a full choice of beans. You can even spice things up with a bonus tot of cognac or whisky (£3). (020-7730 1771; www.tomtom. co.uk; 114 Ebury St, SW1; 8am-5pm Mon-Fri, 9am-6pm Sat & Sun; ; Victoria)

Windsor Castle PUB

22 MAP P156, A3

A classic tavern on the brow of Campden Hill Rd, this place has history, nooks and charm on tap. It's worth the search for its his-toric compartmentalised interior, roaring fire (in winter), delightful beer garden (in summer) and affable regulars (all seasons). According to legend, the bones of Thomas Paine (author of *Rights of Man*) are in the cellar. (www. thewindsorcastlekensington.co.uk; 114 Campden Hill Rd, W11; noon-11pm

Mon-Sat, to 10.30pm Sun; ; Not-ting Hill Gate)

Entertainment

Royal Albert Hall CONCERT VENUE

This splendid Victorian concert hall (see 8 Map p156, D4) hosts classical music, rock and other performances, but is famously the venue for the BBC-sponsored Proms. Booking is possible, but from mid-July to mid-September Proms punters queue for £5 standing (or 'promenading') tickets that go on sale one hour before curtain-up. Otherwise, the box office and prepaid-ticket collection counter are through door 12 (south side of the hall). (0845 401 5034; www.royalalbert-thall.com; Kensington Gore, SW7; South Kensington)

606 Club BLUES, JAZZ

23 MAP P156, F6

Named after its old address on the King's Rd that cast a spell over jazz lovers London-wide back in the '80s, this fantastic, tucked-away basement jazz club and restaurant gives centre stage to contemporary British-based jazz musicians nightly. The club can only serve alcohol to nonmembers who are dining, and it is highly advisable to book to get a table. (020-7352 5953; www.606club. co.uk; 90 Lots Rd, SW10; 7-11.15pm Sun-Thu, 8pm-12.30am Fri & Sat; Imperial Wharf)

Shopping

John Sandoe Books   BOOKS

24 🔒 MAP P156, F6

The perfect antidote to impersonal book superstores, this atmospheric three-storey bookshop in 18th-century premises is a treasure trove of literary gems and hidden surprises. It's been in business for six decades and loyal customers swear by it, while knowledgeable booksellers spill forth with well-read pointers and helpful advice. (📞020-7589 9473; www.johnsandoe.com; 10 Blacklands Tce, SW3; ⊗9.30am-6.30pm Mon-Sat, 11am-5pm Sun; ⊖Sloane Sq)

Harrods   DEPARTMENT STORE

25 🔒 MAP P156, F4

Garish and stylish in equal measure, perennially crowded Harrods is an obligatory stop for visitors, from the cash-strapped to the big spenders. The stock is astonishing, as are many of the price tags. High on kitsch, the 'Egyptian Elevator' resembles something out of an Indiana Jones epic, while the memorial fountain to Dodi and Di (lower ground floor) merely adds surrealism. (📞020-7730 1234; www.harrods.com; 87-135 Brompton Rd, SW1; ⊗10am-9pm Mon-Sat, 11.30am-6pm Sun; ⊖Knightsbridge)

Harvey Nichols   DEPARTMENT STORE

26 🔒 MAP P156, F3

At London's temple of high fashion, you'll find Chloé and Balenciaga bags, the city's best denim range, a massive make-up hall with exclusive lines and great jewellery. The food hall and in-house restaurant, **Fifth Floor**, are, you guessed it, on the 5th floor. From 11.30am to midday, it's browsing time only. (www.harveynichols.com; 109-125 Knightsbridge, SW1; ⊗10am-8pm Mon-Sat, 11.30am-6pm Sun; ⊖Knightsbridge)

Walking Tour 🚶

A Saturday in Notting Hill

A Saturday in Notting Hill sees the neighbourhood at its busiest and best. Portobello Market is full of vibrant colour and the area is stuffed with excellent restaurants, pubs, shops and cinemas, making the entire day an event that embraces market browsing, the culinary, the grain and grape and, last but not least, a chance to catch a film in a classic picture-house setting.

Getting There

🚇 Notting Hill Gate station is on the Circle, District and Central Lines.

🚇 Ladbroke Grove station on the Hammersmith & City and Circle Lines is also useful.

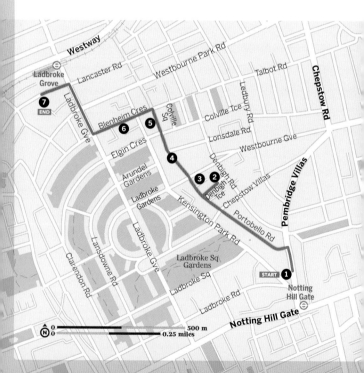

❶ Stock up on Snacks

Conveniently located close to Notting Hill Gate tube station and on the way to Portobello Market, you can't miss **Arancina** (www.arancina.co.uk; mains £3-23.50; ☉8am-11pm Mon-Sat, 9am-11pm Sun) with its orange cut-out Fiat 500 in the window. It's a great spot for *arancini* or a slice of freshly baked pizza.

❷ A Splash of Colour

Divert into **Denbigh Terrace** for a row of vibrantly painted terraced houses on the south side of the street which make for a perfect photo-op, especially if the sun is beaming. The houses make a superb line-up in pink, blue, yellow, grey and other pastel shades.

❸ Earl of Lonsdale

The **Earl of Lonsdale** (☉noon-11pm Mon-Fri, 10am-11pm Sat, noon-10.30pm Sun) is peaceful during the day, with a mixture of old biddies and young hipsters inhabiting its charming snugs. There are Samuel Smith's ales and a fantastic backroom with sofas, banquettes and open fires, as well as a fine beer garden shaded by a towering tree of whopping girth.

❹ Browse the Market

Stroll along Portobello Rd until you reach the iconic **Portobello Road Market** (www.portobellomarket.org; ☉8am-6.30pm Mon-Wed, Fri & Sat, to 1pm Thu). The market mixes street food with fruit and veg, antiques, colourful fashion and trinkets.

❺ Catch a Film (& a Burger)

Wander back down Portobello Rd, where the one-of-a-kind **Electric Cinema** (www.electriccinema.co.uk; tickets £8-22.50) is one of the UK's oldest cinemas, with luxurious leather armchairs, footstools, sofas and even front-row double beds! When the credits roll, head to **Honest Burgers** (www.honestburgers.co.uk; mains from £8.50; ☉11.30am-11pm Mon-Sat, to 10pm Sun, brunch 9.30am-1pm Sat & Sun; 🛜) next door for terrific bites.

❻ Blenheim Crescent

Turn left into Blenheim Cres for a string of browse-worthy shops, including all manner of spices and herbs at the **Spice Shop** (www.thespiceshop.co.uk), eye-catching glassware at **Ceramica Blue** (www.ceramicablue.co.uk; ☉10am-6.30pm Mon-Sat, noon-5pm Sun) and the **Notting Hill Bookshop** (www.thenottinghillbookshop.co.uk; ☉9am-7pm Mon-Sat, 10am-6pm Sun), the inspiration behind the shop in Hugh Grant and Julia Roberts' rom-com *Notting Hill*.

❼ Explore a Museum

Further up Portobello Rd, take a left to the unexpected **Museum of Brands, Packaging & Advertising** (www.museumofbrands.com; adult/child £9/5; ☉10am-6pm Mon-Sat, 11am-5pm Sun), which retraces the history of consumer culture, will have kids amused and parents (and grandparents) all nostalgic over the retro packaging and iconic products from days gone by.

Explore ◈

Regent's Park & Camden

Regent's Park, Camden Market and Hampstead Heath should top your list for excursions into North London. Camden is a major sight with an intoxicating energy and brilliant nightlife, while Regent's Park is an oasis of calm and sophistication amid the North London buzz. Meanwhile, Hampstead Heath (p180) offers you a glorious day out and an insight into how North Londoners spend their weekends.

Start your day with a morning exploration of Regent's Park (p175) and the riveting ZSL London Zoo (p174). In Camden Town, nibble your way around an eclectic variety of snacks at Camden Market (p174). Further explore the markets before rewarding yourself with a delectable ice cream from Chin Chin Labs (p176), or by sitting in the beer garden of the Edinboro Castle (p177) for an afternoon drink. For dinner, opt for Indian delights at Namaaste Kitchen (p177) or reel in some fish and chips at Hook Camden Town (p176). The rest of the night is easily sewn up: Camden has some tremendous pubs and a glut of live-music options embracing most musical persuasions.

Getting There & Around

🚇 For Regent's Park, Baker St (on the Jubilee, Metropolitan, Circle, Hammersmith & City and Bakerloo Lines) is most useful. The best stations for Camden are Camden Town and Chalk Farm on the Northern Line. Hampstead is also on the Northern Line.

Regent's Park & Camden Map on p172

Shops on Camden High St   VALDIS SKUDRE/SHUTTERSTOCK ©

Walking Tour 🥾

Highlights of North London

Part of the appeal of North London is that it's a great area to just wander – in parks, along canals, in markets. This itinerary takes in some of the most atmospheric spots, as well as the big-hitting sights. If you can, stay into the evening to enjoy Camden's fantastic live-music scene.

Walk Facts

Start Madame Tussauds;
🚇 Baker St

End Lock Tavern;
🚇 Chalk Farm

Length 3.8km; 2½ hours

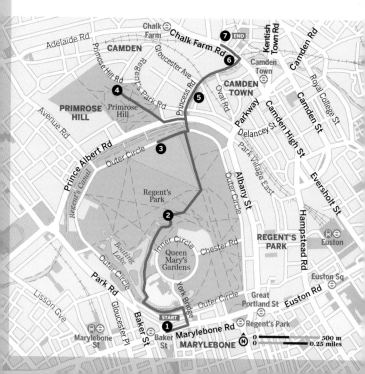

❶ Madame Tussauds

Make sure you pack your selfie stick for a chance to pause with your idols at this waxwork museum (p174) – there are plenty of personalities to admire, from past and current statesmen to sportspeople, actors, singers and movie characters.

❷ Regent's Park

Walk down Marylebone Rd, turn left onto York Gate and head into Regent's Park (p175) – follow the shores of the **boating lake** to explore the most scenic parts of the park before crossing over towards the **Broadwalk**, the park's main avenue.

❸ London Zoo

Explore London's famous zoo (p174), where enclosures have been developed to be as close to the animals' original habitats as possible – among the highlights are Penguin Beach, Tiger Territory, Butterfly Paradise, Gorilla Kingdom and Land of the Lions.

❹ Views from Primrose Hill

Cross Regent's Canal and make your way towards the top of Primrose Hill (p175) for fab views of London's skyline. The park is very popular with families and picnicking revellers at the weekend.

❺ Regent's Canal

Head back down Primrose Hill and join the picturesque Regent's Canal towpath for an amble towards Camden. The path is lined with residential narrow boats and old warehouses converted into modern flats. Leave the towpath when you reach Camden Lock and its market.

❻ Camden Market

Browse the bags, clothes, jewellery and arts and crafts stalls of Camden's famous market. There are three main market areas, but they all sell more or less the same things. Camden Lock Market (p179) is the original; push into Stables Market (p179) for more rummaging.

❼ Restorative Drink

Settle in for a well-earned drink at the Lock Tavern (p178) – if the weather is good, sit on the roof terrace and watch the world go by. Check out what's on in the evening too, as the pub hosts regular bands and DJs.

✕ Take a Break

Camden Market (p174) is packed full of takeaway stalls offering a dazzling array of world cuisines – from French crêpes to Chinese, Argentine grills and sushi, it's all there. Those with a sweet tooth should make a beeline for **Chin Chin Labs** (p176) and its liquid-nitrogen ice creams.

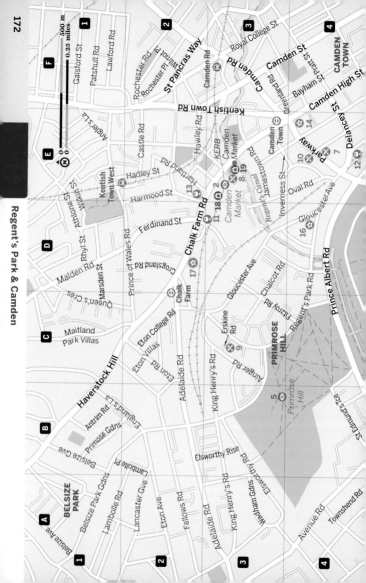

Regent's Park & Camden

0.25 miles
500 m

BELSIZE PARK

Galsford St
Patshull Rd
Lawford Rd

Rochester Rd
Rochester Pl
Willful Rd
St Pancras Way

Royal College St
Camden Rd
Camden St
Camden St
Camden High St

CAMDEN TOWN

Bayham Pratt Rd
Greenland Rd
Camden St
Delancey St

Kentish Town Rd

Castle Rd
Hawley Rd
Hartland Rd
Queen's Rd

KERB
Camden
Market

Camden
Town

Parkway

14
7
12
10

Kentish Town West
Athlone St
Wilkin St
Rhyl St

Hadley St
Harmood St
Ferdinand St
Chalk Farm Rd

13
11 18 2
8·19

Camden
Market
Inverness St
Oval Rd

Regent's Canal
Jamestown Rd

Gloucester Ave

16

Malden Rd
Marsden St
Queen's Cres
Prince of Wales Rd
Crogsland Rd

17

Chalk
Farm

Gloucester Ave
Chalcot Rd
Fitzroy Rd
Regent's Park Rd

Gloucester Ave

Maitland
Park Villas

Haverstock Hill

Eton College Rd
Eton Villas
Eton Rd

Erskine
Rd

9

PRIMROSE
HILL

5

Primrose
Hill

Prince Albert Rd

Antrim Rd
Primrose Gdns
Lambolle Pl
England's La

BELSIZE
PARK

Belsize Ave
Belsize Gve
Lancaster Gve
Lambolle Rd
Belsize Park Gdns

Eton Ave
Fellows Rd
Adelaide Rd

King Henry's Rd
Adelaide Rd
King Henry's Rd
Wedham Gdns

Elsworthy Rise

Anger Rd

Elsworthy Rd

Avenue Rd
Townshend Rd
St Edmund's Tce

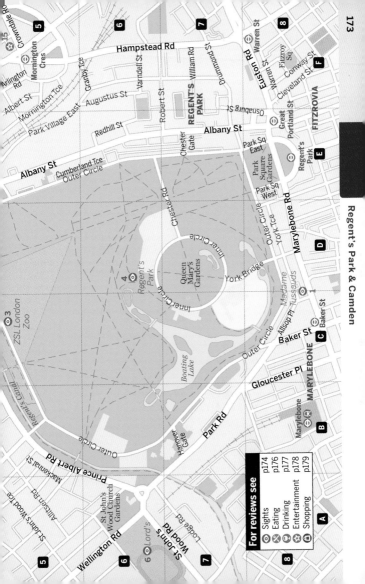

Hampstead Rd

Crowndale Rd

Arlington Rd

Albert St

Mornington Tce

Mornington Cres

Park Village East

Augustus St

Granby Tce

Varndell St

Redhill St

Robert St

REGENT'S PARK

Chester Gate

William Rd

Drummond St

Osnaburgh St

Great Portland St

Euston Rd

Warren St

Warren St

Fitzroy Sq

Conway St

Cleveland St

FITZROVIA

Albany St

Cumberland Tce

Outer Circle

Albany St

Chester Rd

Park Sq East

Park Square Gardens

Park Sq West

Outer Circle

York Tce

Marylebone Rd

Regent's Park

Inner Circle

Queen Mary's Gardens

Regent's Park

York Bridge

Madame Tussauds

ZSL London Zoo

Regent's Canal

Boating Lake

Outer Circle

Allsop Pl

Baker St

Baker St

MARYLEBONE

Gloucester Pl

Marylebone

Marylebone

Prince Albert Rd

Mackennal St

Outer Circle

Hanover Gate

Park Rd

St John's Wood Church Gardens

Lord's

Wellington Rd

St John's Wood Rd

Lodge Rd

Prince Albert Rd

St John's Tce

Allitsen Rd

A5 B5 C5
A6 B6 C6
A7 B7 C7
A8 B8 C8
D E F

Sights

Madame Tussauds · MUSEUM

1 ⊙ MAP P172, C8

It may be kitschy and pricey, but
Madame Tussauds makes for a
fun-filled day. There are photo ops
with your dream celebrity (be it
Daniel Craig, Lady Gaga, Benedict
Cumberbatch, Audrey Hepburn
or the Beckhams), the Bollywood
gathering (sparring studs Hrithik
Roshan and Salman Khan) and the
Royal Appointment (the Queen,
Harry, William and Kate). Book
online for much cheaper rates and
check the website for seasonal
opening hours. (📞0870 400 3000;
www.madame-tussauds.com/london;
Marylebone Rd, NW1; adult/child 4-15yr
£35/30; ⊙10am-6pm; ⊖Baker St)

Camden Market · MARKET

2 ⊙ MAP P172, E3

Although – or perhaps because
– it stopped being cutting-edge
several thousand cheap leather
jackets ago, Camden Market attracts millions of visitors each year
and is one of London's most popular attractions. What started out
as a collection of attractive craft
stalls beside Camden Lock on the
Regent's Canal now extends most
of the way from Camden Town
tube station to Chalk Farm tube
station. (www.camdenmarket.com;
Camden High St, NW1; ⊙10am-6pm;
⊖Camden Town, Chalk Farm)

ZSL London Zoo · ZOO

3 ⊙ MAP P172, C5

Established in 1828, this 15-hectare
zoo is among the oldest in the
world. The emphasis nowadays
is firmly placed on conservation,
education and breeding, with fewer
animals and bigger enclosures.
Highlights include **Land of the
Lions**, **Gorilla Kingdom**, **Tiger
Territory**, the walk-through **In with
the Lemurs** and **Butterfly Paradise**. Feeding sessions and talks
take place throughout the day. The
zoo also organises various experiences, such as Keeper for a Day or
sleepovers in the Bug House. (www.
zsl.org/zsl-london-zoo; Outer Circle, Regent's Park, NW1; adult/child £29.75/22;
⊙10am-6pm Apr-Sep, to 5.30pm Mar &
Oct, to 4pm Nov-Feb; 👶; 🚌274)

North London Neighbourhoods

North London is a collection of small neighbourhoods, originally
ancient villages that were slowly drawn into London as the metropolis expanded. It's a very green area, home to some of the most
wonderful park spaces in the city. Sights are pretty scattered in
the northern half of the area, where you'll need some leg power to
explore hilly Hampstead and around. A walk along Regent's Canal
will link Regent's Park, Camden and King's Cross.

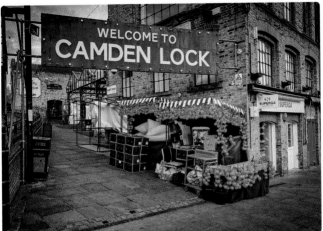

Camden Lock Market (p179)

Regent's Park PARK

4 ⊙ MAP P172, D6

The most elaborate and formal of London's many parks, Regent's Park is one of the capital's loveliest green spaces. Among its many attractions are London Zoo, **Regent's Canal**, an ornamental lake, and sports pitches where locals meet to play football, rugby and volleyball. **Queen Mary's Gardens**, towards the south of the park, are particularly pretty, especially in June when the roses are in bloom. Performances take place here in an **open-air theatre** (☎ 0844 826 4242; www.openairtheatre.org; Queen Mary's Gardens, Regent's Park, NW1; ⊙ May-Sep; ⊕; ⊖ Baker St) during summer. (www.royalparks.org.uk; ⊙ 5am-dusk; ⊖ Regent's Park, Baker St)

Primrose Hill PARK

5 ⊙ MAP P172, B3

On summer weekends, Primrose Hill park is absolutely packed with locals enjoying a picnic and the extraordinary views over the city skyline. Come weekdays, however, and there are mostly just dog walkers and nannies. It's a lovely place to enjoy a quiet stroll or an alfresco sandwich. (⊖ Chalk Farm)

Lord's STADIUM

6 ⊙ MAP P172, A6

The 'home of cricket' is a must for any devotee of this particularly English game. Book early for the Test matches here, but cricket buffs should also take the absorbing and anecdote-filled

Walking along Regent's Canal

The canals that were once a trade lifeline for the capital have now become a favourite escape for Londoners, providing a quiet walk away from traffic and crowds. You can walk from Little Venice to Camden in less than an hour; on the way, you'll pass Regent's Park, London Zoo, Primrose Hill, beautiful villas designed by architect John Nash as well as redevelopments of old industrial buildings into trendy blocks of flats. Allow 15 to 20 minutes between Camden and Regent's Park, and 25 to 30 minutes between Regent's Park and Little Venice. There are plenty of exits on the way and signposts all along.

100-minute tour of the ground and facilities (online booking required). Tours take in the famous Long Room, where members watch the games surrounded by portraits of cricket's great and good, and a museum featuring evocative memorabilia that will appeal to fans old and new. (☏020-7616 8500; www.lords.org; St John's Wood Rd, NW8; tours adult/child £20/12; ☉4-6 tours daily; ⊖St John's Wood)

Eating

Hook Camden Town
FISH & CHIPS £

7 ⊗ MAP P172, E4

In addition to working entirely with sustainable small fisheries and local suppliers, Hook makes all its sauces on-site and wraps its fish in recycled materials, supplying diners with extraordinarily fine-tasting morsels. Totally fresh, the fish arrives in panko breadcrumbs or tempura batter, with seaweed salted chips. Craft beers and fine wines are also on hand. (www.hookrestaurants.com; 65 Parkway, NW1; mains £8-12; ☉noon-3pm & 5-10pm Mon-Thu, noon-10.30pm Fri & Sat, to 9pm Sun; ♿; ⊖Camden Town)

Chin Chin Labs
ICE CREAM £

8 ⊗ MAP P172, E3

This is food chemistry at its absolute best. Chefs prepare the ice-cream mixture and freeze it on the spot by adding liquid nitrogen. Flavours change regularly and match the seasons (spiced hot cross bun, passionfruit and coconut, for instance). Sauces and toppings are equally creative. Try the ice-cream sandwich if you can: ice cream wedged inside gorgeous brownies or cookies. (www.chinchinlabs.com; 49-50 Camden Lock Pl, NW1; ice cream £4-5; ☉noon-7pm; ⊖Camden Town)

Manna
VEGETARIAN ££

9 ⊗ MAP P172, C3

Tucked away on a side street, this upmarket little place does a brisk trade in inventive vegetarian and vegan cooking. The menu features mouth-watering, beautifully presented dishes incorporating elements of Californian, Mexican and Asian cuisine with nods to the raw-food trend. The cheesecake of the day is always a hit. (📞020-7722 8028; www.mannav.com; 4 Erskine Rd, NW3; mains £8-15; ⏰noon-3pm & 6.30-10pm Tue-Sat, noon-7.30pm Sun; 📷; 🚇Chalk Farm)

Namaaste Kitchen INDIAN ££

10 🍴 MAP P172, E4

Although everything's of a high standard, if there's one thing you should try at Namaaste, it's the kebab platter: the meat and fish coming off the kitchen grill are beautifully tender and incredibly flavoursome. The bread basket is another hit, with specialities such as spiced *missi roti* making a nice change from the usual naan. (📞020-7485 5977; www. namaastekitchen.co.uk; 64 Parkway, NW1; mains £10.50-19; ⏰noon-3pm & 5.30-11pm Mon-Fri, noon-11pm Sat & Sun; 📷; 🚇Camden Town)

Drinking

Proud Camden BAR

11 🚇 MAP P172, D3

Proud occupies a former horse hospital within Stables Market, with private booths in the old stalls, fantastic artworks on the walls (the main bar acts as a gallery during the day) and a kooky garden terrace complete with a hot tub. It's also one of Camden's best music venues, with live bands and DJs most nights (entry free to £15). (www.proudcamden.com; Stables Market, Chalk Farm Rd, NW1; ⏰11am-1.30am Mon-Sat, to midnight Sun; 🚇Chalk Farm)

Edinboro Castle PUB

12 🚇 MAP P172, E4

Large and relaxed Edinboro offers a refined atmosphere, gorgeous furniture perfect for slumping into, a fine bar and a full menu. The highlight, however, is the huge beer garden, complete with warm-weather barbecues and decorated with coloured lights on long summer evenings. Patio

---

Camden Market Snacks 🍽️

There are dozens of food stalls at Camden Lock Market, courtesy of food collective **KERB** (Map p172, E3; www.kerbfood.com; Camden Lock Market; mains £6-8; ⏰noon-5pm; 📷; 🚇Camden Town), and at Stables Market (p179), where you can find virtually every type of cuisine, from French to Argentinian, Japanese and Caribbean. Quality varies but is generally pretty good and affordable, and you can eat on the large communal tables, or by the canal.

North London Sounds 👍

North London is the home of indie rock, and many a famous band started out playing in the area's grungy bars. You can be sure to find live music of some kind every night of the week. A number of venues are multi-purpose, with gigs in the first part of the evening (generally around 7pm or 8pm), followed by club nights beginning around midnight.

heaters come out in winter. (www.edinborocastlepub.co.uk; 57 Mornington Tce, NW1; ⏰noon-11pm Mon-Sat, noon-10.30pm Sun; 📶; ⊖Camden Town)

Lock Tavern   PUB

13 🚇 MAP P172, E2

A Camden institution, the black-clad Lock Tavern rocks: it's cosy inside, and there's a rear beer garden and a great roof terrace from where you can watch the market throngs. Beer is plentiful here and it proffers a prolific roll call of guest bands and well-known DJs at weekends to rev things up. Dancing is encouraged. Entry is always free. (www.lock-tavern.com; 35 Chalk Farm Rd, NW1; ⏰noon-midnight Mon-Thu, to 1am Fri & Sat, to 11pm Sun; ⊖Chalk Farm)

Entertainment

Jazz Cafe   LIVE MUSIC

14 ⭐ MAP P172, E4

The name would have you think jazz is the main staple, but it's only a small slice of what's on offer. The intimate clublike space also serves up funk, hip-hop, R&B, soul and rare groove, with big-name acts regularly dropping in. Saturday club night is soul night, with two live sets from the house band. (📞020-7485 6834; www.the-jazzcafelondon.com; 5 Parkway, NW1; ⏰live shows from 7pm, club nights 10pm-3am; ⊖Camden Town)

KOKO   LIVE MUSIC

15 ⭐ MAP P172, F5

Once the legendary Camden Palace, where Charlie Chaplin, the Goons and the Sex Pistols performed, and where Prince played surprise gigs, KOKO is maintaining its reputation as one of London's better gig venues. The theatre has a dance floor and decadent balconies, and attracts an indie crowd. There are live bands most nights and hugely popular club nights on Saturdays. (www.koko.uk.com; 1a Camden High St, NW1; ⊖Mornington Cres)

Cecil Sharp House   TRADITIONAL MUSIC

16 ⭐ MAP P172, D4

If you've ever fancied clog stamping, hanky waving or bell jingling, this is the place for you. Home to the English Folk Dance and Song Society, this institute keeps all manner of wacky folk traditions alive, with performances and classes held in its gorgeous mural-covered Kennedy Hall. The dance classes are oodles of fun; no experience necessary. (www.cecilsharphouse.org; 2 Regent's Park Rd, NW1; ⊖Camden Town)

Roundhouse
CONCERT VENUE

17 ⭐ MAP P172, D2

Built as a railway repair shed in 1847, this unusual Grade II–listed round building became an arts centre in the 1960s and hosted legendary bands before falling into near-dereliction in 1983. Its 21st-century resurrection as a creative hub has been a great success and it now hosts everything from big-name concerts to dance, circus, stand-up comedy, poetry slams and improvisation. (www.roundhouse.org.uk; Chalk Farm Rd, NW1; ⊖Chalk Farm)

Shopping

Stables Market
MARKET

18 🔒 MAP P172, E3

Connected to the Lock Market, the Stables is the best part of the Camden Market complex, with antiques, Asian artefacts, rugs, retro furniture and clothing. As the name suggests, it used to be an old stables complex, complete with horse hospital, where up to 800 horses (who worked hauling barges on Regent's Canal) were housed. (www.camdenmarket.com; Chalk Farm Rd, NW1; ⊙10am-6pm; ⊖Chalk Farm)

Camden Lock Market
MARKET

19 🔒 MAP P172, E3

Right next to the canal lock, this is the original Camden Market, with diverse food stalls, ceramics, furniture, oriental rugs, musical instruments and clothes. (www.camdenmarket.com; 54-56 Camden Lock Pl, NW1; ⊙10am-6pm; ⊖Camden Town)

Walking Tour 🥾

Walking on Hampstead Heath

Sprawling Hampstead Heath, with its rolling woods and meadows, feels a million miles away – despite being approximately four – from central London. Covering 320 hectares, it's home to about 180 bird species, 23 species of butterflies, grass snakes, bats, a rich array of flora and expansive views from the top of Parliament Hill. North Londoners adore this vast green expanse and it's particularly busy with families, dog walkers and picnickers.

Getting There

🚇 Hampstead station is on the Northern Line. For Highgate Cemetery, get off at Archway (Northern Line).

🚌 Hampstead Heath and Gospel Oak are at the heath's south end.

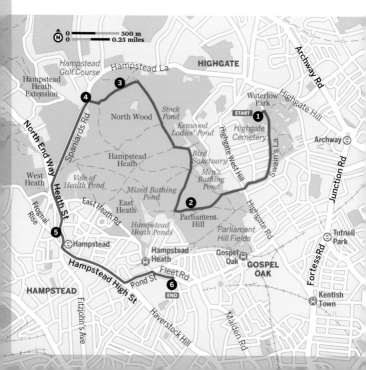

❶ Explore the Local Cemetery

The final resting place of Karl Marx, George Eliot and Russian secret service agent Alexander Litvinenko (the latter poisoned with radioactive polonium-210 in 2006), **Highgate Cemetery** (www.highgatecemetery.org; adult/child £4/free; ⏱10am-4pm Mon-Fri, 11am-4pm Sat & Sun) is divided into East and West. To visit the atmospheric West Cemetery, you must take a tour.

❷ Parliament Hill

From the cemetery head down Swain's Lane to the Highgate West Hill roundabout and climb to Parliament Hill for all-inclusive views south over town. Londoners adore picnicking here – choose your spot, tuck into some sandwiches and feast on the superb vistas. If the weather is warm, you could even swim at the **Hampstead Heath Ponds** (www.cityoflondon.gov.uk; adult/child £2/1; ⊖Hampstead Heath) (open year-round, lifeguard-supervised).

❸ Visit Kenwood

Traverse the heath to the magnificent neoclassical 18th-century **Kenwood** (www.english-heritage.org.uk; Hampstead Lane, NW3; admission free; ⏱10am-4pm) in a glorious sweep of perfectly landscaped gardens leading down to a picturesque lake. The house contains a magnificent collection of art, including paintings by Rembrandt, Constable and Turner. Seek out the **Henry Moore** and **Barbara Hepworth sculptures** in the grounds, too.

❹ Rest at the Spaniard's Inn

At the heath's edge is this marvellous 1585 tavern, where Byron, Shelley, Keats and Dickens all paused for a tipple. Once a toll house, the **Spaniard's Inn** (www.thespaniardshampstead.co.uk; ⏱noon-11pm) has kept its historic charm – wood panelling, jumbled interior and hearty welcome – and is hugely popular with dog walkers, families and other park revellers on weekends.

❺ Mooch around Hampstead

After a restorative pint at the Spaniard's Inn, take bus 210 to Jack Straw's Castle stop and walk down to the historic neighbourhood of Hampstead, a delightful corner of London. Loved by artists in the interwar years, it has retained a bohemian feel, with sumptuous houses, leafy streets, cafes and lovely boutiques. Try **Exclusivo** (2 Flask Walk, NW3; ⏱10.30am-6pm) for top-quality, secondhand designer garments.

❻ Dinner at the Stag

Finish your day with a stroll down to the **Stag** (www.thestagnw3.com; mains £9-17.50; ⏱noon-11pm), a fine gastropub where you'll be rewarded with delicious British fare. The beef and ale pie is one of a kind and the desserts are stellar. The wine and beer selection will ensure you're in no rush to go home.

Explore ◉

Shoreditch &
the East End

Shoreditch and Spitalfields make up in atmosphere and history for what they lack in 'big ticket sights'. Here you'll encounter poignant reminders of the capital's long history of migration and some of London's most intriguing house museums. The area is also the heart of London's creative industry, and feels like it is actively shaping the next chapter in London's history.

Begin your day exploring historic Clerkenwell, joining a tour of ancient Charterhouse (p187). Pop over to fun, superbly presented Poppie's (p188) for a traditional fish and chips lunch. Unless you can get tickets for a candlelit evening visit to Dennis Severs' House (p187), stop by to explore its particular magic. Stop by Old Spitalfields Market (p191), amble around the streets of Georgian Spitalfields (p188) and wander down vibrant Brick Lane (p187) and grab a bite at Brick Lane Beigel Bake (p189). Line up a drink at the Cocktail Trading Co (p189) or the Queen of Hoxton (p190). For comfortable time out from treading paving slabs, check out a film at the Electric Cinema (p190), or feast at Brawn (p188).

Getting There & Around

◉ Liverpool St is the closest tube stop to Spitalfields. Old St is the best stop for the western edge of Hoxton and Shoreditch.

🚌 Shoreditch High St and Hoxton are the closest stations to Spitalfields and the eastern parts of Shoreditch and Hoxton.

🚌 Useful buses include routes 55, 8 and 242.

Shoreditch & the East End Map on p186

Pitfield Street, Hoxton, *Art Thief* by STIK ANDY KIRBY/MRKIRBY/500PX ©

Walking Tour 🥾

A Sunday in the East End

The East End has a colourful and multicultural history. Waves of migrants (French Protestant, Jewish, Bangladeshi) have left their mark on the area, which, added to the Cockney heritage and the 21st-century hipster phenomenon, has created an incredibly vibrant neighbourhood. It's best appreciated on Sundays, when the area's markets are in full swing.

Walk Facts

Start Columbia Road Flower Market; ⊖Hoxton

End Yuu Kitchen; ⊖Aldgate East

Length 1.2km, three to four hours, depending on stops

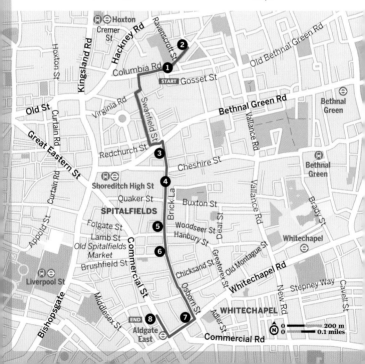

❶ Columbia Rd Flower Market

This weekly **market** (www.columbia road.info; ⏰8am-3pm Sun) sells an amazing array of flowers and plants. It's a lot of fun and the best place to hear proper Cockney barrow-boy banter. It gets packed, so go early.

❷ Pub Break

Escape the crush in the wood-lined confines of the **Royal Oak** (www. royaloaklondon.com; ⏰4-11pm Mon-Fri, noon-midnight Sat, 11am-10.30pm Sun), a lovely old East End pub with a little garden out the back.

❸ Grab a Bagel

Brick Lane was once the centre of the Jewish East End. Much of the Jewish community has moved to other areas but the no-frills **Brick Lane Beigel Bake** (p189) still does a roaring trade in dirt-cheap homemade bagels.

❹ Brick Lane Market

This street is best known for its huge Sunday **market** (www.visitbrick-lane.org; ⏰10am-5pm Sun). You'll find anything from vintage to bric-a-brac, cheap fashion and food stalls.

❺ Designer Stalls at the Old Truman Brewery

Founded here in the 17th century, Truman's Black Eagle Brewery was, by the 1850s, the largest brewery in the world. Spread over a series of brick buildings and yards straddling both sides of Brick Lane, the complex now hosts edgy markets, including the funky **Sunday Up-Market** (www.sundayupmarket.co.uk; ⏰11am-6pm Sat, 10am-5pm Sun), featuring young fashion designers.

❻ Brick Lane Great Mosque

No building symbolises the different waves of immigration to Spitalfields quite as well as this **mosque** (www.bricklanejammemasjid.co.uk). Built in 1743 as the New French Church for the Huguenots, it was a Methodist chapel from 1819 until it was transformed into the Great Synagogue for Jewish refugees from Russia and central Europe in 1898. In 1976 it changed faiths yet again, becoming the Great Mosque.

❼ Art at Whitechapel Gallery

This ground-breaking **gallery** (www.whitechapelgallery.org; admission free; ⏰11am-6pm Tue, Wed & Fri-Sun, to 9pm Thu) doesn't have a permanent collection but is devoted to hosting contemporary art exhibitions. It made its name by staging exhibitions by both established and emerging artists, including the first UK shows by Pablo Picasso and Frida Kahlo.

❽ Yuu Kitchen

The East End is known for its multi-ethnic restaurants, so end your day with a Pan-Asian feast. Manga images pout on the walls and birdcages dangle from the ceiling at this fun, relaxed **eatery** (www.yuukitchen.com; dishes £4.50-8.50; ⏰5.30pm-late Mon & Tue, noon-2.30pm & 5.30pm-late Wed-Fri, noon-4pm & 5.30pm-late Sat & Sun). Don't miss the show-stopping *bao* (Taiwanese steamed buns).

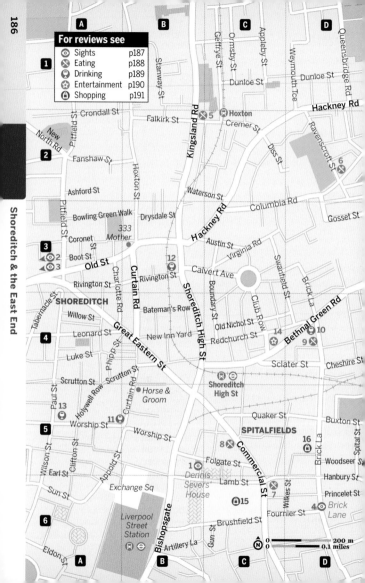

Shoreditch & the East End

For reviews see

◉	Sights	p187
✖	Eating	p188
🍷	Drinking	p189
★	Entertainment	p190
🔒	Shopping	p191

Sights

Dennis Severs' House

MUSEUM

1 ◎ MAP P186, B5

This extraordinary Georgian House is set up as if its occupants – a family of Huguenot silk weavers – had just walked out the door. There are half-drunk cups of tea and partially consumed food, lit candles and, in perhaps unnecessary attention to detail, a full chamber pot by the bed. More than a museum, it's an opportunity to meditate on the minutiae of everyday Georgian life through silent exploration.

Bookings are required for the evening Silent Night candlelit sessions (every Monday, Wednesday and Friday from 5pm to 9pm), but you can just show up for the daytime sessions. Visits take around 45 minutes. (☏020-7247 4013; www.dennissevershouse.co.uk; 18 Folgate St, E1; day/night £10/15; ⌚noon-2pm & 5-9pm Mon, 5-9pm Wed & Fri, noon-4pm Sun; ⊖Liverpool St)

Charterhouse

HISTORIC BUILDING

2 ◎ MAP P186, A3

From a monastery, to a Tudor mansion, to the charitable foundation that's operated here since 1611, Charterhouse has played a discreet but important part in London's story. Visitors have free access to the small museum, the chapel and the main court, but must join a one-hour tour to see more (£10 and well worth it).

These run three times daily and take in the most historic rooms and courts, and the cloister. (☏020-7253 9503; www.thecharterhouse.org; Charterhouse Sq, EC1M; admission free; ⌚11am-5pm Tue-Sun; ⊖Barbican)

St John's Gate

HISTORIC BUILDING

3 ◎ MAP P186, A3

This remarkable Tudor gate dates from 1504. During the 12th century, the Knights Hospitaller (a Christian and military order with a focus on providing care to the sick) established a priory here. Inside is a small museum that covers the history of the order (including rare examples of the knights' armour), as well as its 19th-century revival in Britain as the Christian Order of St John and the foundation of St John Ambulance. (www.museumstjohn.org.uk; St John's Lane, EC1M; admission free; ⌚10am-5pm daily Jul-Sep, Mon-Sat Oct-Jun; ⊖Farringdon)

Brick Lane

STREET

4 ◎ MAP P186, D6

Full of noise, colour and life, Brick Lane is a vibrant mix of history and modernity, and a palimpsest of cultures. Today it is the centrepiece of a thriving Bengali community in an area nicknamed Banglatown. The southern part of the lane is one long procession of curry and balti houses intermingled with fabric shops and Indian supermarkets. (⊖Shoreditch High St, Liverpool St)

Georgian Spitalfields

Crowded around its famous market and grand parish church, Spitalfields has long been one of the capital's most multicultural areas. Waves of Huguenot (French Protestant), Jewish, Irish and, more recently, Indian and Bangladeshi immigrants have made Spitalfields home. To get a sense of what Georgian Spitalfields was like, branch off to Princelet, Fournier, Elder and Wilkes Streets. Having fled persecution in France, the Huguenots set up shop here from the late 17th century, practising their trade of silk weaving.

Eating

Sông Quê   VIETNAMESE £

5 ⊗ MAP P186, B2

With the kind of demand for seats that most London restaurants can only dream of, this no-frills, hospital-green Vietnamese joint has been feeding the denizens of London for almost 15 years and often has a queue of people waiting. Service can be abrupt but the food is spot on, with two dozen types of fantastic *pho* (noodle soup) to choose from. (www.songque. co.uk; 134 Kingsland Rd, E2; mains £7.20-9.50; ◷ noon-3pm & 5.30-11pm Mon-Fri, noon-11pm Sat, to 10.30pm Sun; ⊖ Hoxton)

Brawn   EUROPEAN ££

6 ⊗ MAP P186, D2

There's a French feel to this relaxed corner bistro, yet the menu wanders into Italian and Spanish territory as well, and even tackles that British institution, the Sunday lunch (three courses £28). Dishes are seasonally driven and delicious,

and there's an interesting selection of European wine on offer. (☎ 020-7729 5692; www.brawn.co; 49 Columbia Rd, E2; mains £14-19; ◷ noon-3pm Tue-Sat, 6-10.30pm Mon-Thu, to 11pm Fri & Sat, noon-4pm Sun; ⊖ Hoxton)

Poppie's   FISH & CHIPS ££

7 ⊗ MAP P186, C6

This glorious re-creation of a 1950s East End chippy comes complete with waitstaff in pinnies and hairnets, and Blitz memorabilia. As well as the usual fishy suspects, it does old-time London staples – jellied eels and mushy peas – plus kid-pleasing, sweet-tooth desserts (sticky toffee pudding or apple pie with ice cream), and there's a wine list. (www.poppiesfishandchips.co.uk; 6-8 Hanbury St, E1; mains £12.20-16.90; ◷ 11am-11pm; ⊖ Liverpool St)

Hawksmoor   STEAK £££

8 ⊗ MAP P186, C5

You could easily miss discreetly signed Hawksmoor, but confirmed carnivores will find it worth seeking out. The dark wood, bare bricks and velvet curtains make for a handsome setting in which to gorge yourself on the best of British beef. The Sunday roasts (£20) are legendary. (☎020-7426 4850; www.thehawksmoor.com; 157 Commercial St, E1; mains £20-50; ⏱noon-2.30pm & 5-10.30pm Mon-Sat, noon-9pm Sun; 🔊; ⊖Liverpool St)

Brick Lane Beigel Bake BAKERY £

9 ❌ MAP P186, D4

This relic of the Jewish East End still makes a brisk trade serving dirt-cheap homemade bagels (filled with salmon, cream cheese and/or salt beef) to hungry shoppers and late-night boozers. The queues on Sundays are epic.

(159 Brick Lane, E2; bagels £1-4.10; ⏱24hr; ⊖Shoreditch High St)

Drinking

Cocktail Trading Co COCKTAIL BAR

10 🚇 MAP P186, D4

In an area famous for its edgy, don't-give-a-damn attitude, this exquisite cocktail bar stands out for its classiness and cocktail confidence. The drinks are truly unrivalled, from the flavours to the presentation – bottles presented in envelopes, ice cubes as big as a Rubik's cube and so on. The decor is reminiscent of a colonial-era gentlemen's club, just warmer and more welcoming. (www.thecocktailtradingco.co.uk; 68 Bethnal Green Rd, E1; ⏱5pm-midnight Mon-Fri, 2pm-midnight Sat, 2-10.30pm Sun; 🚇Shoreditch High St)

Salt beef bagel

Queen of Hoxton BAR

11 🍺 MAP P186, A5

This industrial-chic bar has a games room, basement and varied music nights (including oddballs such as dance lessons and ukulele jamming sessions), but the real drawcard is the vast rooftop bar, decked out with flowers, fairy lights and even a wigwam. It has fantastic views across the city. (www.queenofhoxton.com; 1 Curtain Rd, EC2A; ⏰4pm-midnight Mon-Wed, to 2am Thu-Sat; 🛜; 🚇Liverpool St)

Cargo BAR, CLUB

12 🍺 MAP P186, B3

Cargo is one of London's most eclectic clubs. Under its brick railway arches you'll find a dance floor, a bar and an outside terrace adorned with two original Banksy images. The music policy (hip-hop, pop, R&B and club classics) is varied, with plenty of up-and-coming bands also in the line-up. Food is available throughout the day. (www.cargo-london.com; 83 Rivington St, EC2A; ⏰noon-1am Mon-Thu, to 3am Fri & Sat, to midnight Sun; 🚇Shoreditch High St)

Worship Street Whistling Shop COCKTAIL BAR

13 🍺 MAP P186, A5

While the name is Victorian slang for a place selling illicit booze, this subterranean drinking den's master mixologists explore the experimental limits of cocktail chemistry and aromatic science, as well as concocting the classics. Many ingredients are made with rotary evaporators in the on-site lab. (📞020-7247 0015; www.whistlingshop.com; 63 Worship St, EC2A; ⏰5pm-midnight Mon & Tue, to 1am Wed & Thu, to 2am Fri & Sat; 🚇Old St)

Entertainment

Electric Cinema CINEMA

14 ⭐ MAP P186, C4

Run by Shoreditch House, an uberfashionable private member's club, this is cinema-going that

Fancy a Late One?

Pubs and clubs **333 Mother** (Map p186, B3; www.333mother.com; 333 Old St, EC1V; ⏰noon-2.30am Sun-Thu, to 3am Fri & Sat; 🚇Old St), **XOYO** (www.xoyo.co.uk; 32-37 Cowper St, EC2A; ⏰10pm-3am Mon, Tue & Thu, 9.30pm-4am Fri & Sat; 🚇Old St), **Cargo** (reviewed above) and the **Horse & Groom** (Map p186, B5; www.thehorseandgroom.net; 28 Curtain Rd, EC2A; ⏰11.30am-11pm Mon-Wed, to 2am Thu, to 4am Fri, 6pm-4am Sat; 🚇Shoreditch High St) all stay open until at least 3am on weekends. For breakfast with a pint, the **Fox & Anchor** (p123) throws back its doors at 7am (8.30am on weekends).

Drinking Directions

Shoreditch is the torch bearer of London's nightlife: there are dozens of bars, clubs and pubs, open virtually every night of the week (and until the small hours at weekends) and it can get pretty rowdy. Clerkenwell is more sedate, featuring lovely historic pubs and fine cocktail bars. Spitalfields sits somewhere in between the two extremes and tends to be defined by its City clientele on week nights and market-goers on Saturday and Sunday.

will impress a date, with space for an intimate 48 on the comfy armchairs. There's a full bar and restaurant in the complex, and you can take your purchases in with you. Tickets go like crazy, so book ahead. (📞020-3350 3490; www. electriccinema.co.uk; 64-66 Redchurch St, E2; tickets £11-19; 🚉Shoreditch High St)

Shopping

Old Spitalfields Market   MARKET

15 🅰 MAP P186, C6

Traders have been hawking their wares here since 1638 and it's still one of London's best markets. Today's covered market was built in the late 19th century, with the more modern development added in 2006. Sundays are the biggest and best days, but Thursdays are good for antiques and Fridays for independent fashion. There are plenty of food stalls too. (www. oldspitalfieldsmarket.com; Commercial St, E1; ⏲10am-5pm Mon-Fri & Sun, 10am-6pm Sat; 🚇Liverpool St)

Rough Trade East   MUSIC

16 🅰 MAP P186, D5

It's no longer directly associated with the legendary record label (home to The Smiths, The Libertines and The Strokes, among many others), but this huge record shop is still the best for music of an indie, soul, electronica and alternative persuasion. In addition to an impressive selection of CDs and vinyl, it also dispenses coffee and stages promotional gigs. (www. roughtrade.com; Old Truman Brewery, 91 Brick Lane, E1; ⏲9am-9pm Mon-Thu, to 8pm Fri, 10am-8pm Sat, 11am-7pm Sun; 🚉Shoreditch High St)

Worth a Trip 🔭

Royal Observatory & Greenwich Park

The Royal Observatory is where the study of the sea, the stars and time converge. The prime meridian charts its line through the grounds of the observatory, chosen quite arbitrarily in 1884, to divide the globe into the eastern and western hemispheres. The observatory sits atop a hill within leafy and regal Greenwich Park, London's oldest royal park.

www.rmg.co.uk

Greenwich Park,
Blackheath Ave, SE10

adult/child £10/6.50, incl
Cutty Sark £20/11.50

🕐 10am-5pm Sep-Jun,
to 6pm Jul & Aug

🚉 DLR Cutty Sark, DLR
Greenwich, Greenwich

Flamsteed House

Charles II ordered construction of the Christopher Wren–designed Flamsteed House, the original observatory building, on the foundations of Greenwich Castle in 1675 after closing the observatory at the Tower of London. Today it contains the magnificent **Octagon Room** and the rather simple apartment where the astronomer royal and his family lived. Below are the brilliant **Time Galleries** explaining how the longitude problem – how to accurately determine a ship's east-west location – was solved through astronomical means and the invention of the chronometer.

Meridian Courtyard

In the Meridian Courtyard, where the globe is decisively sliced into east and west, visitors can delightfully straddle both hemispheres, with one foot on either side of the meridian line. Every day the red Time Ball at the top of the Royal Observatory drops at 1pm, as it has done ever since 1833. There's also a telescope on a platform with amazing views over London, and a map of what you can see.

Camera Obscura

Situated in a small brick summerhouse next to the Meridian Courtyard, this astonishing **room** (www.rmg.co.uk; Greenwich Park; ⏰10am-5pm) projects a live image of Queen's House – and the people moving in front of it and the boats on the Thames behind – onto a table. Enter through two layers of thick curtains – to keep the light out; make sure you close them behind you to keep the room as dark as possible.

Weller Astronomy Galleries

The southern half of the observatory contains the highly informative (and free) Weller Astronomy Galleries, where you can touch the

★ **Top Tips**

○ Choose a sunny day for the astonishing views from the observatory across London.

○ See the website for combination tickets with other Greenwich sights and membership, which can save money.

○ Visit nearby Queen's House (p195) afterwards, with its beautiful Tulip Stairs and the Great Hall.

✕ **Take a Break**

You're spoiled for choice for break stops. There's a cafe at the Astronomy Centre or you can devour a sandwich in Greenwich Park.

Alternatively, head downhill to **Goddards at Greenwich** (www.goddardsat greenwich.co.uk; 22 King William Walk, SE10; dishes £3.30-7.30; ⏰10am-7pm Sun-Thu, to 8pm Fri & Sat) for some pie 'n' mash or snack your way around nearby Greenwich Market (p197).

Free Access Areas

Unlike most other attractions in Greenwich, the Royal Observatory contains free-access areas (such as Weller Astronomy Galleries) and ones you pay for (Meridian Line, Flamsteed House and Camera Obscura).

oldest object you will ever encounter: part of the **Gibeon meteorite**, a mere 4.5 billion years old! Other engaging exhibits include an orrery (mechanical model of the solar system, minus the as-yet-undiscovered Uranus and Neptune) from 1780, astronomical documentaries, a first edition of Newton's *Principia Mathematica* and the opportunity to view the Milky Way in multiple wavelengths. This is also the venue of the annual **Insight Astronomy Photographer of the Year** exhibition, with its astonishing images. To take stargazing further, pick up a Skyhawk telescope from the shop.

Peter Harrison Planetarium

The state-of-the-art Peter Harrison Planetarium – London's only planetarium – can cast entire heavens onto the inside of its roof. It runs at least five informative shows a day. Booking advised.

Greenwich Park

This is one of London's loveliest expanses of **green** (www.royalparks.org.uk; King George St, SE10; ⊖ 6am-around sunset; ⎇ Greenwich, Maze Hill, DLR Cutty Sark), with a **rose garden**, picturesque walks, Anglo-Saxon tumuli

Greenwich Park

Ground Zero

The Greenwich meridian was selected as the global prime meridian at the International Meridian Conference in Washington DC in 1884. Greenwich became the world's ground zero for longitude and standard for time calculations, replacing the multiple meridians that had existed till then. Greenwich was assisted in its bid by the earlier US adoption of Greenwich Mean Time for its own national time zones. In any case, the majority of world trade already used sea charts that identified Greenwich as the prime meridian.

and astonishing views from the crown of the hill near the **Statue of General Wolfe** towards Canary Wharf – the financial district across the Thames. Covering 74 hectares, it's the oldest enclosed royal park and is partly the work of André Le Nôtre, the landscape architect who designed the palace gardens of Versailles.

The park contains a lovely **teahouse** near the Royal Observatory, a cafe behind the National Maritime Museum, a **deer park**, tennis courts in the southwest and a boating lake at the **Queen's House** (www.rmg.co.uk/queens-house; ⊙ Romney Rd, SE10; admission free; ⊗ 10am-5pm; ℞ DLR Cutty Sark) end. There's also **Ranger's House** (Wernher Collection; EH; ☎ 020-8294 2548; www.english-heritage.org.uk; Greenwich Park, Chesterfield Walk, SE10; adult/child £9/5.40; ⊗ guided tours 11.30am & 2pm Sun-Wed late Mar-Sep) and the park is full of chestnut trees – head there in October and pick the nuts from the ground.

Walking Tour 🥾

A Wander Around Historic Greenwich

The top sight in regal riverside Greenwich is the Royal Observatory, but the neighbourhood is a treasure-trove of sights, from the grand Old Royal Naval College to the exquisite perfection of Queen's House, a magnificent 19th-century clipper ship, noteworthy church architecture, a historic market, riverside pubs and a walk beneath the river.

Getting There

🚈 Take the DLR to Cutty Sark or Greenwich, or the train to Greenwich.

⚓ Thames Clippers boats run to Greenwich and Royal Arsenal Woolwich from the London Eye, Embankment and Tower Millennium piers.

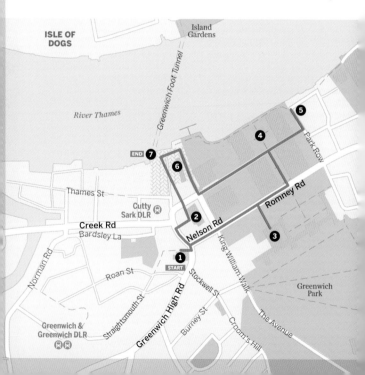

❶ St Alfege Church

From Greenwich & Greenwich DLR station, stroll down Greenwich High Rd to this Nicholas Hawksmoor-designed **church** (www.st-alfege. org; ⏱11am-4pm Mon-Fri, 10am-4pm Sat, noon-4pm Sun) dating to 1718, featuring a restored mural by James Thornhill and an intriguing keyboard from the Tudor period with middle keyboard octaves. Free concerts take place at 1.05pm on Thursdays and most Saturdays.

❷ Shop & Snack around Greenwich Market

Cross the road to **Greenwich Market** (⏱10am-5.30pm), established in 1737, and snack your way through its eclectic street eats, after perusing the stalls selling crafts, wholesome mass products, hand-made jewellery, cool fashion pieces, antiques and more. Check the website for what's for sale on which day.

❸ National Maritime Museum & Queen's House

Walk along Nelson Rd to the **National Maritime Museum** (www. rmg.co.uk/national-maritime-museum; admission free; ⏱10am-5pm), one of Greenwich's standout attractions. After exploring the collection, cross to the recently restored **Queen's House** (p195), the most graceful building in Greenwich.

❹ Old Royal Naval College

Cross Romney Rd to the outstanding **Old Royal Naval College** (www.

ornc.org; admission free; ⏱10am-5pm, grounds 8am-11pm), Greenwich's grandest collection of buildings. The views to Canary Wharf are stunning, while the main draws are the **Chapel** and the **Painted Hall** (the latter is closed for restoration work, though tours are available; see the website).

❺ Sink a Pint in the Trafalgar Tavern

Exit via the East Gate and head down Park Row to this marvellous old waterside **pub** (www.trafalgar-tavern.co.uk; ⏱noon-11pm Mon-Thu, noon-midnight Fri, 10am-midnight Sat, 10am-11pm Sun) with big windows overlooking the Thames. Dickens apparently knocked back a few here – and used it as the setting for the wedding breakfast scene in *Our Mutual Friend*.

❻ Catch the *Cutty Sark*

Follow the scenic riverside path between the Thames and the Old Royal Naval College to the **Cutty Sark** (www.rmg.co.uk/cuttysark; King William Walk, SE10; adult/child £13.50/7; ⏱10am-5pm Sep-Jun, to 6pm Jul & Aug), the last of the great clipper ships to sail between China and England in the 19th century.

❼ Cross under the River on Foot

Descend to the **Greenwich Foot Tunnel** (Cutty Sark Gardens, SE10; ⏱24hr; 🚇DLR Cutty Sark) and cross under the river to the Isle of Dogs for stupefying views of Greenwich from the far shore.

Worth a Trip 🔭
Hampton Court Palace

London's most spectacular Tudor palace, 16th century Hampton Court Palace is steeped in history, from the grand living quarters of Henry VIII to the spectacular gardens, complete with a 300-year-old maze. One of the best days out London has to offer, the palace is mandatory for anyone with an interest in British history, Tudor architecture or gorgeous landscaped gardens. Set aside plenty of time to do it justice.

www.hrp.org.uk/
hamptoncourtpalace

adult/child/family
£19/10/34

🕐 10am-4.30pm Nov-Mar,
to 6pm Apr-Oct

Entering the Palace

Passing through the magnificent main gate, you arrive first in the **Base Court** and beyond that **Clock Court**, named after its 16th-century astronomical clock. The panelled rooms and arched doorways in the **Young Henry VIII Exhibition** upstairs from Base Court provide a rewarding introduction: note the Tudor graffiti on the fireplace. Off Base Court to the right as you enter, and acquired by Charles I in 1629, Andrea Magenta's nine-painting series **The Triumphs of Caesar** portray Julius Caesar returning to Rome in a triumphant procession.

Henry VIII's State Apartments

The stairs inside Anne Boleyn's Gateway lead up to Henry VIII's Apartments, including the stunning **Great Hall**. The **Horn Room**, hung with impressive antlers, leads to the **Great Watching Chamber** where guards controlled access to the king.

Royal Pew & Henry VIII's Crown

Henry VIII's dazzling gemstone-encrusted crown has been re-created – the original was melted down by Oliver Cromwell – and sits in the Royal Pew (open 10am to 4pm Monday to Saturday and 12.30pm to 1.30pm Sunday), which overlooks the beautiful **Chapel Royal** (still a place of worship after 450 years).

Tudor Kitchens & Great Wine Cellar

Also dating from Henry's day are the delightful Tudor kitchens, once used to rustle up meals for a royal household of some 1200 people. Don't miss the Great Wine Cellar, which handled the 300 barrels each of ale and wine consumed here annually in the mid-16th century.

★ Top Tips

o Check on the website to see what activities are on when you visit and join a tour with a costumed guide!

o Hampton Court presses up against 445-hectare Bushy Park, a semi-wild expanse with herds of red and fallow deer.

✗ Take a Break

There are three cafes within the grounds of the palace: the **Tiltyard Cafe**, the **Privy Kitchen** and the **Fountain Court Cafe**. The gardens of the palace are huge, so pack a picnic and lie on the grass, if it's sunny.

★ Getting There

Hampton Court Palace is one hour southwest of central London.

Regular services from Waterloo to Hampton Court via Wimbledon Station.

Boats from Westminster Pier take around four hours.

Cumberland Art Gallery

The restored Cumberland Suite off Clock Court is the venue for a staggering collection of art works from the Royal Collection, including Rembrandt's *Self-Portrait in a Flat Cap* (1642) and Sir Anthony van Dyck's *Charles I on Horseback* (c 1635–6).

William III's & Mary II's Apartments

A tour of William III's Apartments, completed by Wren in 1702, takes you up the grand **King's Staircase**. Highlights include the **King's Presence Chamber**, dominated by a throne backed with scarlet hangings. The sumptuous **King's Great Bedchamber**, with a bed topped with ostrich plumes, and the King's Closet (where His Majesty's toilet has a velvet seat) should not be missed. Restored and recently reopened, the unique **Chocolate Kitchens** were built for William and Mary in about 1689.

William's wife Mary II had her own apartments, accessible via the fabulous **Queen's Staircase** (decorated by William Kent).

Georgian Private Apartments

The Georgian Rooms were used by George II and Queen Caroline on the court's last visit to the palace in 1737. Do not miss the fabulous Tudor **Wolsey Closet** with its early 16th-century ceiling and painted panels, commissioned by Henry VIII.

Kitchen, Hampton Court Palace

Events & Activities

Check the schedule for spectacular shows and events, including Tudor jousting, falconry displays, ghost hunts (for children), garden adventures and family trails. In summer, fun 15- to 20-minute shire-horse-drawn **charabanc tours** (adult/child £6/3) depart from the East Front Garden between 11am and 5pm. Luna Cinema (www.theluna-cinema.com) hosts outdoor films in summer at the palace. From late November to mid-January you can glide (or slide) around the palace's glittering ice rink.

Cartoon Gallery

The Cartoon Gallery used to display the original Raphael Cartoons (now in the V&A Museum); nowadays it's just the late-17th-century copies.

Gardens & Maze

Beyond the palace are the stunning gardens; keep an eye out for the **Real Tennis Court**, dating from the 1620s. Originally created for William and Mary, the **Kitchen Garden** is a magnificent re-creation.

No one should leave Hampton Court without losing themselves in the **800m-long maze** (⊙10am-5.15pm Apr-Oct, to 3.45pm Nov-Mar; adult/child/family £4.20/2.60/12.30), also accessible to those not entering the palace.

Survival Guide

Before You Go

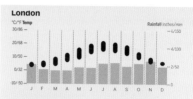

Book Your Stay

○ Great neighbour-hoods to stay in include around the National Gallery and Covent Garden, Kensington, St Paul's and the City, and the South Bank.

○ Bed and breakfasts come in a tier below hotels, but can have boutique style charm, a lovely old building setting and a personal level of service.

○ There are some fantastic hotels in London, but demand can often outstrip supply, especially at the bottom end of the market, so book ahead, particularly during holiday periods and in summer.

○ For less than £100 per night you'll be limited to mostly B&Bs and hostels. Look out, though, for weekend deals in City hotels that can put a better class of hotel within reach.

○ If you're in London for a week or more, a

When to Go

○ **Winter (Dec–Feb)** Cold, short days with much rain and occasional snow. Museums and at-tractions quieter.

○ **Spring (Mar–May)** Mild, wet, trees in blos-som. Major sights begin to get busy and parks start to look lovely.

○ **Summer (Jun–Aug)** Warm to hot, sunny with long days. Main tourist and holi-day season. Sights can be crowded, but parks are lovely.

○ **Autumn (Sep–Nov)** Mild, sunny, good-looking season. Kids back at school. London quietens down after summer.

short term or serviced apartment can be economical and give you more of a sense of living in the city.

Useful Websites

Visit London (www.visitlondon.com) Huge range of listings from the city's official tour-ism portal.

London Town (www.londontown.com) Excellent last-minute offers on boutique hotels and B&Bs.

Alastair Sawdays (www.sawdays.co.uk) Hand-picked selec-tion of boltholes in the capital.

Lonely Planet (www.lonelyplanet.com/london) Hundreds of properties.

Best Budget

YHA London Oxford Street (www.yha.org.uk/hostel/london-oxford-street) Centrally positioned hostel with excellent shared facilities.

Qbic (www.qbichotels.
com) Well-designed lit-
tle rooms available at
a steal if booked early
enough.

Clink78 (www.clinkhos-
tels.com/london/clink78)
Heritage hostel in a
former magistrates
court.

Best Midrange

**citizenM Tower of
London** (www.citizenm.
com) Small but per-
fectly formed rooms,
some with killer views.

Hoxton Hotel (www.
thehoxton.com) Out-
standing value for its
location and design.

40 Winks
(www.40winks.org)
Whimsically deco-
rated boutique B&B in
the East End.

Barclay House (www.
barclayhouselondon.com)
Ticks every box – and
a few more.

Best Top End

Hazlitt's (www.hazlitts
hotel.com) Old-world
elegance in a terrific
location.

South Place (www.
southplacehotel.com)
Artsy boutique offer-
ing on the edge of the
City.

Knightsbridge Hotel
(www.firmdalehotels.com/
hotels/london/knights-
bridge-hotel) Elegant
rooms in a 200-year-
old house.

Corinthia (www.corin-
thia.com) Victorian jewel
in the crown near the
seat of power.

Arriving
in London

Heathrow Airport

Some 15 miles west of
central London, Heath-
row Airport (LHR;
www.heathrowairport.
com) is one of the
world's busiest inter-
national airports and
counts four passenger
terminals (numbered
2 to 5), including the
revamped Terminal 2.
It's Britain's main air-
port for international
flights.

Underground Three
Underground stations
on the Piccadilly line
serve Heathrow:
one for Terminals 2
and 3, another for
Terminal 4, and the
terminus for Terminal
5. The Underground,
commonly referred

to as 'the tube', is
the cheapest way of
getting to Heathrow;
paper tickets cost
one-way £6, Oyster
or Contactless peak/
off-peak £5.10/3.10.
The journey to central
London takes one
hour and trains
depart every three
to nine minutes. Leav-
ing from the airport,
it runs from just
after 5am to just after
midnight (11.28pm
Sunday), and head-
ing to the airport it
runs from 5.09am to
11.54pm (11pm on
Sunday); tube trains
run all night Friday
and Saturday, with
reduced frequency.
Buy tickets at the
station.

Train Heathrow
Express, every 15
minutes, and Heath-
row Connect, every
30 minutes, trains link
Heathrow with Pad-
dington train station.
Heathrow Express
trains take a mere
15 minutes to reach
Paddington. Trains
on each service run
from around 5am and
between 11pm and
midnight.

Bus National Express
(www.nationalex-
press.com) Coaches

(one-way from £6, 35 to 90 minutes, every 30 minutes to one hour) link the Heathrow Central bus station with London Victoria coach station. The first bus leaves the Heathrow Central bus station (at Terminals 2 and 3) at 4.20am, with the last departure just after 10pm. The first bus leaves Victoria at 3am, the last at around 12.30am. At night, the N9 bus (£1.50, 1¼ hours, every 20 minutes) connects Heathrow Central bus station (and Heathrow Terminal 5) with central London, terminating at Aldwych.

Taxi A metered black-cab trip to/from central London will cost between £46 and £87 and take 45 minutes to an hour, depending on traffic and your departure point.

Gatwick Airport

Located some 30 miles south of central London, Gatwick (LGW; www.gatwick-airport.com) is smaller than Heathrow and is Britain's number-two airport, mainly for international flights. The North and South Terminals are linked by a 24-hour shuttle train, with the journey time about three minutes.

Train National Rail (www.nationalrail.co.uk) has regular train services to/from London Bridge (30 minutes, every 15 to 30 minutes), London King's Cross (55 minutes, every 15 to 30 minutes) and London Victoria (30 minutes, every 10 to 15 minutes). Fares vary depending on the time of travel and the train company, but allow £10 to £20 for a single.

○ Gatwick Express trains run every 15 minutes from the station near the Gatwick South Terminal to London Victoria. From the airport, there are services between 5.45am and 12.20am. From Victoria, they leave between 5am and 11.30am. The journey takes 30 minutes.

Bus National Express (www.national express.com) Coaches run throughout the day from Gatwick to London Victoria coach station (one way from £8). Services depart hourly around the clock. Journey time is between 80 minutes and two hours, depending on traffic.

○ EasyBus (www.easybus.co.uk) Runs 19-seater minibuses to Gatwick every 15 to 20 minutes on several routes, including from Earl's Court/West Brompton and Victoria coach station (one way from £1.95). The service runs round the clock. Journey time averages 75 minutes.

Taxi A metered black-cab trip to/from central London costs around £100 and takes just over an hour. Minicabs are usually cheaper.

Stansted Airport

Stansted (STN; www.stanstedairport.com) is 35 miles northeast of central London in the direction of Cambridge. An international airport, Stansted serves a multitude of mainly European destinations and is served primarily by low-cost carriers such as Ryanair.

Train Stansted Express (www.stanstedexpress.com) rail service (45 minutes, every 15 to 30 minutes) links the airport and Liverpool St station. From the airport, the first train leaves at 5.30am, the last at 12.30am. Trains depart Liverpool St station from 3.40am to 11.25pm.

Bus National Express (www.nationalexpress.com) coaches run around the clock, offering well over 100 services per day.

○ Airbus A6 runs to Victoria coach station (around one hour to 1½ hours, every 20 minutes) via Marble Arch, Paddington, Baker St and Golders Green. Airbus A7 also runs to Victoria coach station (around one hour to 1½ hours, every 20 minutes), via Waterloo and Southwark. Airbus A8 runs to Liverpool St station (one way from £6, 60 to 80 minutes, every 30 minutes), via Bethnal Green, Shoreditch High St and Mile End.

○ Stansted City Link 767 runs to London King's Cross every 30 minutes and takes 75 minutes.

○ Airport Bus Express runs every 30 minutes to London Bridge, Victoria coach station, Liverpool Street and Stratford.

○ EasyBus (www.easybus.co.uk) runs services to Baker St and Old St tube stations every 15 minutes. The journey (one way from £4.95) takes one hour from Old St, 1¼ hour from Baker St.

○ Terravision (www.terravision.eu) coaches link Stansted to Liverpool St train station (one way from £9, 55 minutes), King's Cross (from £9, 75 minutes) and Victoria coach station (from £10, two hours) every 20 to 40 minutes between 6am and 1am. Wi-fi on all buses.

Taxi A metered black cab trip to/from central London costs around £130. Minicabs are cheaper.

St Pancras International Station

Eurostar (www.eurostar.com) high-speed passenger rail service linking London St Pancras International with Paris, Brussels and Lille. It has up to 19 daily departures. Fares vary greatly, from £29 one way standard class to around £245 one way for a fully flexible business premier ticket (prices based on return journeys). There are deals on Eurostar Snap, with best value fares for those with flexibility around the specific train they travel on.

Getting Around

Public transport in London is excellent, if pricey. It's managed by Transport for London (www.tfl.gov.uk), which has a great, multilingual website with live updates on traffic, a journey planner, maps and detailed information on all modes of transport. The cheapest way to travel across the network is with an Oyster card or a contactless card. Children under 11 travel free.

Oyster Card

The Oyster Card is a smart card on which you can store credit towards 'prepay' fares, as well as Travelcards valid for periods from a day to a year. Oyster Cards are valid across the entire public transport network in London.

All you need to do when entering a station is touch your card on a reader (which has a yellow circle with the image of an Oyster Card on it) and then touch again on your way out. The system will then deduct the appropriate amount of credit from your card, as necessary. For bus journeys, you only need to touch once upon boarding. Note that some train stations don't have exit turnstiles, so you will need to tap out on the reader before leaving the station; if you forget, you will be hugely overcharged.

The benefit lies in the fact that fares for Oyster Card users are lower than standard ones. If you are making many journeys during the day, you will never pay more than the appropriate Travelcard (peak or off-peak) once the daily 'price cap' has been reached.

Oyster Cards can be bought (£5 refundable deposit required) and topped up at any Underground station, travel information centre or shop displaying the Oyster logo. To get your deposit back along with any remaining credit, simply return your Oyster Card at a ticket booth.

Contactless cards (which do not require chip and pin or a signature) can now be used directly on Oyster Card readers and are subject to the same Oyster fares. The advantage is that you don't have to bother with buying, topping up and then returning an Oyster Card, but foreign visitors should bear in mind the cost of card transactions.

Underground, DLR & Overground

The **London Underground** ('the tube'; 11 colour-coded lines) is part of a system that also includes the Docklands Light Railway (DLR; www.tfl.gov.uk/dlr; a driverless overhead train operating in the eastern part of the city) and Overground network (mostly outside of Zone 1 and sometimes underground).

It is the quickest and easiest way of getting around the city, but it's not cheap. It's always cheapest to travel with an Oyster Card or a contactless card than a paper ticket.

First trains operate from around 5.30am Monday to Saturday and 6.45am Sunday. The last trains leave around 12.30am Monday to Saturday and 11.30pm Sunday.

Selected lines (the Victoria and Jubilee lines, plus most of the Piccadilly, Central and Northern lines) run all night on Friday and

Saturday on what is called the 'Night Tube', with trains running every 10 minutes or so. London is divided into nine concentric fare zones.

Bus

○ Red double-decker buses afford great views of the city, but be aware that the going can be slow.

○ There are excellent bus maps at every stop detailing all routes and destinations served from that particular area.

○ Many bus stops have LED displays listing bus arrival times, but downloading a bus app such as London Bus Live Countdown to your smartphone is the most effective way to keep track of when your next bus is due.

○ Cash cannot be used on London's buses. Instead you must pay with an Oyster Card, Travelcard or a contactless payment card. Bus fares are a flat £1.50, no matter the distance travelled.

○ Bus services normally operate from 5am to 11.30pm.

○ More than 50 night-bus routes (prefixed

with the letter 'N') run from 11.30pm to 5am.

○ Oxford Circus, Tottenham Court Rd and Trafalgar Sq are the main hubs for night routes.

○ Another 60 bus routes operate 24 hours; the frequency decreases between 11pm and 5am.

○ Children under 11 travel free; 11 to 15 year olds are half-price if registered on an accompanying adult's Oyster Card (register at Zone 1 or Heathrow tube stations).

Bicycle

Santander Cycles

(📞 0343 222 6666; www. tfl.gov.uk/modes/cycling/santander-cycles) are straightforward and particularly useful for visitors.

○ Pick up a bike from one of the 750 docking stations dotted around the capital. Drop it off at another docking station.

○ The access fee is £2 for 24 hours. Insert your debit or credit card in the docking station to pay your access fee.

○ The first 30 minutes are free, then it's £2 for any additional

period of 30 minutes (the pricing structure encourages short journeys).

○ Take as many bikes as you like during your access period (24 hours), leaving five minutes between each trip.

○ If the docking station is full, consult the terminal to find available docking points nearby. You must be 18 to buy access and at least 14 to ride a bike.

Taxi

○ Black cabs are available for hire when the yellow sign above the windscreen is lit; just stick your arm out to signal one.

○ Fares are metered, with the flag fall charge of £2.60 (covering the first 248m during a weekday), rising by increments of 20p for each subsequent 124m.

○ Fares are more expensive in the evenings and overnight.

○ You can tip taxi drivers up to 10%, but most Londoners simply round up to the nearest pound.

○ Apps such as mytaxi (https://uk.mytaxi. com/hailo) use your smartphone's GPS to locate the nearest black cab.

○ You only pay the metered fare. ComCab (www.comcab-london. co.uk) operates one of the largest fleets of black cabs in town.

○ Minicabs, which are licensed, are cheaper (usually) competitors of black cabs, but cannot be hailed on the street. They must be hired by phone or directly from one of the minicab offices.

○ Minicabs don't have meters; there's usually a fare set by the dispatcher. Make sure you ask before setting off.

○ Apps such as Kabbee allow you to book a minicab in double-quick time and can save you money.

Boat

○ **Thames Clippers** (www.thamesclippers. com) boats run regular services between Embankment, Waterloo (London Eye), Blackfriars, Bankside (Shakespeare's Globe), London Bridge, Tower Bridge, Canary Wharf, Greenwich, North Greenwich and Woolwich piers (all zones adult/

child £9/4.50), from 6.55am to around midnight (from 9.29am weekends).

○ **Westminster Passenger Services Association** (www. wpsa.co.uk) boats run between April and September to Hampton Court Palace from Westminster Pier in central London (via Kew and Richmond).

○ **London Waterbus Company** (www. londonwaterbus.com) runs canal boats between Camden Lock and Little Venice.

Car & Motorcycle

○ Expensive parking charges, traffic jams, high petrol prices, efficient traffic wardens and wheel-clampers make car hire unattractive for most visitors.

○ There is a congestion charge of £11.50 per day in central London. For full details check www.tfl.gov.uk/roadusers/congestion-charging.

○ **Avis** (www.avis.co.uk), **Hertz** (www.hertz.co.uk) and **easyCar** (www.easycar.com) have several car-rental branches across the capital.

○ It is illegal to use a mobile phone to call or text while driving (using a hands-free device to talk on your mobile is permitted).

○ Cars drive on the left in the UK.

○ All drivers and passengers must wear seat belts and motorcyclists must wear a helmet.

Essential Information

Accessible Travel

○ For travellers with access needs, London is a frustrating mix of user-friendliness and head-in-the-sand disinterest. New hotels and modern tourist attractions are legally required to be accessible to people in wheelchairs, but many historic buildings, B&Bs and guesthouses are in older buildings, which are hard or prohibitively expensive to adapt. Similarly, visitors with vision, hearing or cognitive impairments will find their needs met in a piecemeal fashion.

○ The good news is that as a result of hosting the 2012 Olympics and Paralympics, and thanks to a forward-looking tourist board in VisitEngland, things are improving all the time.

○ Around a quarter of tube stations, half of overground stations, most piers, all tram stops, the Emirates Air Line (cable car) and all DLR stations have step-free access.

○ Buses can be lowered to street level when they stop and wheelchair users travel free.

○ All black cabs are wheelchair-accessible, but power wheelchair users should note that the space is tight and sometimes headroom is insufficient.

○ Guide dogs are universally welcome on public transport and in hotels, restaurants, attractions etc.

Business Hours

Banks 9am to 5pm Monday to Friday

Post offices 9am to 5.30pm Monday to Friday and 9am to noon Saturday

Pubs & bars 11am to 11pm (many are open later)

Restaurants noon to 2.30pm and 6 to 11pm

Shops 9am to 7pm Monday to Saturday, noon to 6pm Sunday

Sights 10am to 6pm

Discount Cards

○ **London Pass** (www.londonpass.com; 1/2/3/6/10 days £62/85/101/139/169) offers free entry and queue jumping at major attractions; check the website for details.

○ Passes can be tailored to include use of the Underground and buses.

Electricity

Type G
230V/50Hz

Emergency

Dial 🕿 999 to call the police, fire brigade or ambulance in an emergency.

Money

○ The unit of currency of the UK is the pound sterling (£).

○ One pound sterling consists of 100 pence (called 'p' colloquially).

○ Notes come in denominations of £5, £10, £20 and £50; coins are 1p, 2p, 5p, 10p, 20p, 50p, £1 and £2.

ATMs

○ Ubiquitous ATMs generally accept Visa, MasterCard, Cirrus or Maestro cards and more obscure ones. There is usually a transaction surcharge for cash withdrawals with foreign cards.

○ Non-bank-run ATMs that charge £1.50 to £2 per transaction are usually found inside shops (and are particularly expensive for foreign-bank card holders). Look for 'Free cash withdrawals' signs to avoid these.

Changing Money

The best place to change money is in any local post-office branch, where no commission is charged.

You can also change money in most high-street banks and some travel agencies, as well as at the numerous bureaux de change throughout the city.

Credit & Debit Cards

○ Credit and debit cards are accepted almost universally in London, from restaurants and bars to shops and even by some taxis.

○ American Express and Diners Club are far less widely used than Visa and MasterCard.

○ Contactless cards and payments (which do not require a chip and pin or a signature) are increasingly

Money-Saving Tips

○ Visit free museums and sights.

○ Buy an Oyster card.

○ Take the bus.

widespread (watch for the wi-fi-like symbol on cards, shops, taxis, buses, the Underground, rail services and other transport options). Transactions are limited to a maximum of £30.

Tipping

○ Many restaurants add a 'discretionary' service charge to your bill – it's legal but should be clearly advertised. In places that don't, you are expected to leave a 10% to 15% tip (unless service was unsatisfactory).

○ No need to tip to have your pint pulled or wine poured in a pub.

Public Holidays

New Year's Day 1 January

Good Friday Late March/April

Easter Monday Late March/April

May Day Holiday First Monday in May

Spring Bank Holiday Last Monday in May

Summer Bank Holiday Last Monday in August

Christmas Day 25 December

Boxing Day 26 December

Safe Travel

○ London's a fairly safe city considering its size, so exercising common sense should keep you safe.

Telephone

○ Some public phones still accept coins, but most take phonecards (available from retailers, including most post offices and some newsagents) or credit cards.

○ British Telecom's famous red phone boxes survive in conservation areas only (notably Westminster).

Calling London

○ London's area code is 020, followed by an eight-digit number beginning with 7 (central London), 8 (Greater London) or 3 (nongeographic). You only need to dial the 020 when you are calling London from elsewhere in the UK or if you're dialling from a mobile.

o To call London from abroad, dial your country's international access code (usually 00 but 011 in Canada and the USA), then 44 (the UK's country code), then 20 (dropping the initial 0), followed by the eight-digit phone number.

International Calls & Rates

o International direct dialling (IDD) calls to almost anywhere can be made from nearly all public telephones.

o International calling cards with stored value (usually £5, £10 or £20) and a PIN, which you can use from any phone by dialling a special access number, are usually the cheapest way to call abroad. These cards are available at most corner shops.

o Note that the use of Skype or Whatsapp may be restricted in some hostels because of noise and/or bandwidth issues.

Mobile Phones

o The UK uses the GSM 900 network, which covers Europe, Australia and New Zealand, but is not compatible with CDMA mobile technology used in the US and Japan (although some American and Japanese phones can work on both GSM and CDMA networks).

o If you have a GSM phone, check with your service provider about using it in the UK and ask about roaming charges.

o It's usually better to buy a local SIM card from any mobile-phone shop, though in order to do that your handset from home must be unlocked.

Tourist Information

Visit London (www. visitlondon.com) can fill you in on everything from attractions and events to tours and accommodation. Kiosks are dotted about the city and can also provide maps and brochures; some branches are able to book theatre tickets.

Heathrow Airport Tourist Information Centre (www. visitlondon.com/tag/ tourist-information-centre; Terminal 1, 2 & 3 Underground station concourse; 7.30am-8.30pm) Information on transport, accommodation, tours and more. You can buy Oyster cards, Travelcards and bus passes here too.

There are other Tourist Information Centres in King's Cross St Pancras Station, Liverpool Street Station, Piccadilly Circus Underground Station, The City, Greenwich and Victoria Station.

Visas

Immigration to the UK is becoming tougher, particularly for those seeking to work or study. Make sure you check www. gov.uk/check-uk-visa, or with your local British embassy, for the most up-to-date information.

Behind the Scenes

Send Us Your Feedback

We love to hear from travellers – your comments help make our books better. We read every word, and we guarantee that your feedback goes straight to the authors. Visit **lonelyplanet.com/contact** to submit your updates and suggestions.

Note: We may edit, reproduce and incorporate your comments in Lonely Planet products such as guidebooks, websites and digital products, so let us know if you don't want your comments reproduced or your name acknowledged. For a copy of our privacy policy visit lonelyplanet.com/privacy.

Damian's Thanks

Many thanks to Ann Harper, Jasmin Tonge, Kevin and Maki Fallows, Rosemary Hadow, Lily Greensmith, Antonia Mavromatidou, Arabella Sneddon, Bill Moran, Jim Peake, my coauthors, and much gratitude again to Daisy, Tim and Emma.

Peter's Thanks

Researching in London is always a joy, due in large part to the company of a great bunch of friends

This Book

This 6th edition of Lonely Planet's *Pocket London* guidebook was curated by Damian Harper and researched and written by Damian along with Peter Dragicevich, Steve Fallon and Emilie Filou. Damian, Peter, Steve and Emilie also wrote the previous edition. This guidebook was produced by the following:

Destination Editors
James Smart, Clifton Wilkinson

Series Designer
Campbell McKenzie

Cartographic Series Designer Wayne Murphy

Associate Product Director Martine Power

Senior Product Editor Genna Patterson

Product Editor Sandie Kestell

Senior Cartographer Mark Griffiths

Book Designer Katherine Marsh

Assisting Editors Katie Connolly, Sam Wheeler

Cover Researcher Brendan Dempsey-Spencer

Thanks to Imogen Bannister, Laura Crawford, Blaze Hadzik, James Hardy, Liz Heynes, Simon Hoskins, Chris Lee Ack, Jean-Pierre Masclef, Anne Mason, Liam McGrellis, Virginia Moreno, Darren O'Connell, Naomi Parker, Kirsten Rawlings, Wibowo Rusli, Dianne Schallmeiner, Ellie Simpson, John Taufa, Angela Tinson, Saralinda Turner, Juan Winata and London-based Lonely Planet writers and editors. Particular thanks go to Kurt Crommelin, Rob Carpenter, Tim Benzie, Paul Joseph, Marcus O'Donnell, Suzannah and Oliver de Montfort, Damian Harper, Emilie Filou, Steve Fallon, Tasmin Waby, Brana Vladisavljevic, Anna Tyler and James Smart for your company and encouragement.

Steve's Thanks

Many thanks to fellow authors Emilie Filou, Damian Harper and Peter Dragicevich for their advice and suggestions along the way. Fellow Blue Badge Tourist Guides – too many to name – were also of great help, especially Lia Lalli. As always, I'd like to state my admiration, gratitude and great love for my partner, Michael Rothschild, especially in this year when wedding bells will peal.

Emilie's Thanks

Big thanks to my friends Catherine, Philippe, Kathleen and Nikki who came along during research and made it so enjoyable. Thanks also to my co-writers Steve, Damian and Peter for all the destination sharing. And finally, thank you to my wonderful husband, Adolfo, for joining me when possible, and our one-and-only Miss Dynamite, aka Sasha, for reminding me that life is all about simple pleasures.

Acknowledgements

Cover photograph: Palace of Westminster, Houses of Parliament and Big Ben, Olimpio Fantuz/4Corners ©

Photographs pp38–9 (from left): alice-photo; Alexey Fedorenko; IR Stone / Shutterstock ©; Pitfield Street, Hoxton, *Art Thief* by STIK, Andy Kirby, mrkirby / 500px ©

Index

See also separate subindexes for:

⊗ **Eating p218**

⊜ **Drinking p219**

✪ **Entertainment p220**

🔒 **Shopping p220**

Steve Fallon

After a full 15 years living in the centre of the known universe – East London – Steve cockney-rhymes in his sleep, eats jellied eel for brekkie, drinks lager by the bucketful and dances around the occasional handbag. As always, he did everything the hard/fun way: walking the walks, seeing the sights, taking (some) advice from friends, colleagues and the odd taxi driver and digesting everything in sight. Steve is a qualified London Blue Badge Tourist Guide.

Emilie Filou

Emilie was born in Paris, where she lived until she was 18. Following her three-year degree and three gap years, she found herself in London, fell in love with the place and never really left. She now works as a journalist specialising in Africa and makes regular trips to the region from her home in northeast London. You can see her work on www.emiliefilou.com; she tweets @EmilieFilou.

Our Writers

Damian Harper

Born off the Strand within earshot of Bow Bells (favourable wind permitting), Damian grew up in Notting Hill way before it was discovered by Hollywood. A onetime Shakespeare and Company bookseller and radio presenter, Damian has been authoring guidebooks for Lonely Planet since the late 1990s. He lives in South London with his wife and two kids, and frequently returns to China (his second home).

Peter Dragicevich

After a dozen years reviewing music and restaurants for publications in New Zealand and Australia, Peter could no longer resist London's bright lights and loud guitars. Like all good Kiwis, he got to know the city while surfing his way between friends' flats all over London before finally putting down roots in North London, although these days he's living back in Auckland, New Zealand.

Published by Lonely Planet Global Limited
CRN 554153
6th edition – Oct 2018
ISBN 978 1 78657 444 2
© Lonely Planet 2018   Photographs © as indicated 2018
10 9 8 7 6 5 4 3 2 1
Printed in Singapore